COMMON SENSE

Yoritomo-Tashi was the founder of the first Japanese dynasty of Shoguns, and one of the greatest statemen Japan has ever had. He was also a well-known philosopher who was admired by his people. He wrote extensively on philosophical subjects, and his ideas are encapsulated in books such as *Common Sense: How to Exercise It* and *The Power of Influence*.

COMMON SENSE
HOW TO EXERCISE IT

Timeless Wisdom from one of Japan's
Greatest Statesmen to have Ever Lived

YORITOMO-TASHI

Published by
Rupa Publications India Pvt. Ltd 2024
7/16, Ansari Road, Daryaganj
New Delhi 110002

Sales centres:
Bengaluru Chennai
Hyderabad Jaipur Kathmandu
Kolkata Mumbai Prayagraj

Edition copyright © Rupa Publications India Pvt. Ltd 2024

All rights reserved.
No part of this publication may be reproduced, transmitted,
or stored in a retrieval system, in any form or by any means,
electronic, mechanical, photocopying, recording or otherwise, without
the prior permission of the publisher.

P-ISBN: 978-93-6156-651-6
E-ISBN: 978-93-6156-055-2

Second impression 2025

10 9 8 7 6 5 4 3 2

Printed in India

This book is sold subject to the condition that it shall not, by way of
trade or otherwise, be lent, resold, hired out, or otherwise circulated,
without the publisher's prior consent, in any form of binding or
cover other than that in which it is published.

CONTENTS

1. Common Sense: What Is It? — 1
2. The Fight Against Illusion — 14
3. The Development of the Reasoning Power — 23
4. Common Sense and Impulse — 35
5. The Dangers of Sentimentality — 46
6. The Utility of Common Sense in Daily Life — 56
7. Power of Deduction — 66
8. How to Acquire Common Sense — 77
9. Common Sense and Action — 92
10. The Most Thorough Business Man — 103
11. Common Sense and Self-Control — 114
12. Common Sense Does Not Exclude Great Aspirations — 123

1

COMMON SENSE: WHAT IS IT?

One beautiful evening, Yoritomo-Tashi was strolling in the gardens of his master, Lang-Ho, listening to the wise counsels which he knew so well how to give in all attractiveness of allegory, when, suddenly, he paused to describe a part of the land where the gardener's industry was less apparent.

Here parasitic plants had, by means of their tendrils, crept up the shrubbery and stifled the greater part of its flowers.

Only a few of them reached the centre of the crowded bunches of the grain stalks and of the trailing vines that interlaced the tiny bands which held them against the wall.

One plant alone, of sombre blossom and rough leaves, was able to flourish even in close proximity to the wild verdure. It seemed that this plant had succeeded in avoiding the dangerous entanglements of the poisonous plants because of its tenacious and fearless qualities, at the same time its shadow was not welcome to the useless and noxious creeping plants.

"Behold, my son," said the Sage, "and learn how to understand the teachings of nature: The parasitic plants represent negligence against the force of which the best of intentions vanish."

Energy, however, succeeds in overcoming these obstacles which increase daily; it marks out its course among entanglements and rises from the midst of the most encumbered centres, beautiful and strong.

Ambition and audacity show themselves also after having passed through thousands of difficulties and having overcome them all.

Common sense rarely needs to strive; it unfolds itself in an atmosphere of peace, far from the tumult of obstructions and snares that are not easily avoided.

Its flower is less alluring than many others, but it never allows itself to be completely hidden through the wild growth of neighbouring branches.

It dominates them easily, because it has always kept them at a distance.

Modest but self-sustaining, it is seen blossoming far from the struggles which always retard the blossoming of plants and which render their flowering slower and, at times, short-lived.

A most absurd prejudice has occasionally considered common sense to be an inferior quality of mind.

This error arises from the fact that it can adapt itself as well to the most elevated conceptions as to the most elemental mentalities.

To those who possess common sense is given the faculty of placing everything in its proper rank.

It does not underestimate the value of sentiments by

attributing to them an exaggerated importance.

It permits us to consider fictitious reasons with reservation and of resolutely rejecting those that resort to the weapons of hypocrisy.

Persons who cultivate common sense never refuse to admit their errors.

One may truly affirm that they are rarely far from the truth, because they practise directness of thought and force themselves never to deviate from this mental attitude.

Abandoning for a moment his favourite demonstration by means of symbolism, Yoritomo said to us:

"Common sense should be thus defined:

"It is a central sense, toward which all impressions converge and unite in one sentiment—the desire for the truth.

"For people who possess common sense, everything is summed up in one unique perception:

"The love of directness and simplicity.

"All thoughts are found to be related; the preponderance of these two sentiments makes itself felt in all resolutions, and chiefly in the reflections which determine them.

"Common sense permits us to elude fear which always seizes those whose judgement vacillates; it removes the defiance of the Will and indicates infallibly the correct attitude to assume."

And Yoritomo, whose mind delighted in extending his observations to the sociological side of the question, adds:

"Common sense varies in its character, according to surroundings and education.

"The common sense of one class of people is not the same as that of a neighbouring class.

"Certain customs, which seem perfectly natural to Japan would offend those belonging to the western world, just as our Nippon prejudices would find themselves ill at ease among certain habits customary among Europeans."

"Common sense," he continues, "takes good care not to assail violently those beliefs which tradition has transmuted into principles.

"However, if direct criticism of those beliefs causes common sense to be regarded unfavourably, it will be welcomed with the greatest reserve and will maintain a certain prudence relative to this criticism, which will be equivalent to a proffered reproach.

"Common sense often varies as to external aspects, dependent upon education, for it is evident that a diamio (Japanese prince) can not judge of a subject in the same way as would a man belonging to the lowest class of society.

"The same object can become desirable or undesirable according to the rank it occupies.

"Must one believe that common sense is excluded from two such incompatible opinions?

"No, not at all. An idea can be rejected or accepted by common sense without violating the principles of logic in the least.

"If, as one frequently sees, an idea be unacceptable because of having been presented before those belonging to a particular environment, common sense, by applying its laws, will recognize that the point of view must be changed before the idea can become acceptable."

And again, Yoritomo calls our attention to a peculiar circumstance.

"Common sense," he says, "is the art of resolving questions, not the art of posing them.

"When taking the initiative it is rarely on trial.

"But the moment it is a case of applying practically that which ingenuity, science or genius have invented, it intervenes in the happiest and most decisive manner.

"Common sense is the principle element of discernment.

"Therefore, without this quality, it is impossible to judge either of the proposition or the importance of the subject.

"It is only with the aid of common sense that it is possible to distinguish the exact nature of the proposition, submitted for a just appreciation, and to render a solution of it which conforms to perfect accuracy of interpretation.

"The last point is essential and has its judicial function in all the circumstances of life. Without accuracy, common sense can not be satisfactorily developed, because it finds itself continually shocked by incoherency, resulting from a lack of exactness in the expression of opinions."

If we wish to know what the principal qualities are which form common sense, we shall turn over a few pages and we shall read:

"Common sense is the synthesis of many sentiments, all of which converge in forming it.

"The first of these sentiments is reason. "Then follows moderation.

"To these one may add:

"The faculty of penetration; "The quality consistency.

"Then, wisdom, which permits us to profit by the lessons of experience.

"A number of other qualities must be added to these,

in order to complete the formation of common sense; but, although important, they are only the satellites of those we have just named.

"Reason is really indispensable to the projection of healthy thoughts.

"The method of reasoning should be the exhaustive study of minute detail, of which we shall speak later.

"For the moment we shall content ourselves by indicating, along the broad lines of argument, what is meant by this word reason.

"Reasoning is the art of fixing the relativeness of things.

"It is by means of reasoning that it is possible to differentiate events and to indicate to what category they belong.

"It is the habit of reasoning to determine that which it is wise to undertake, thus permitting us to judge what should be set aside.

"How could we guide ourselves through life without the beacon-light of reason? It pierces the darkness of social ignorance, it helps us to distinguish vaguely objects heretofore plunged in obscurity, and which will always remain invisible to those who are unprovided with this indispensable accessory—the gift of reasoning.

"He who ventures in the darkness and walks haphazard, finds himself suddenly confronted by obstacles which he was unable to foresee.

"He finds himself frightened by forms whose nature he cannot define, and is often tempted to attribute silhouettes of assassins to branches of trees, instead of recognizing the real culprit who is watching him from the corner of the wild forest.

"Life, as well as the wildest wilderness, is strewn with pitfalls. To think of examining it rapidly, without the aid of that torch called reason, would be imitating the man of whom we have just spoken.

"Many are the mirages, which lead us to mistake dim shadows for disquieting realities, unless we examine them critically, for otherwise we can never ascribe to them their true value.

"Certain incidents, which seem at first sight to be of small importance, assume a primordial value when we have explained them by means of reasoning.

"To reason about a thing is to dissect it, to examine it from every point of view before adopting it, before deferring to it or before rejecting it; in one word, to reason about a thing is to act with conscious volition, which is one of the phases essential to the conquest of common sense.

"This principle conceded, it then becomes a question of seriously studying the method of reasoning, which we propose to do in the following manner but first it is necessary to be convinced of this truth."

Without reason there is no common sense.

Yoritomo teaches us that, although moderation is only of secondary importance, it is still indispensable to the attainment of common sense.

It is moderation which incites us to restrain our impatience, to silence our inexplicable antipathies and to put a break on our tempestuous enthusiasms.

Can one judge of the aspect of a garden while the tempest is twisting the branches of the trees, tearing off the tendrils of the climbing vines, scattering the petals of the flowers and spoiling the corollas already in full bloom?

And now, Yoritomo, who loves to illustrate his teachings by expressive figures of speech, tells us the following story.

"A Japanese prince, on awakening, one day, demanded lazily of his servants what kind of weather it was, but he forbade them to raise the awnings which kept a cool, dim light in his room and shielded his eyes from the strong light from without. The two servants left him reclining upon his divan and went into the adjoining room, where the stained-glass windows were not hung with curtains.

"One of them, putting his face close to a yellow-tinted pane of glass, exclaimed in admiration of the beautiful garden, bathed in the early morning sunlight.

"The second one, directing his gaze to a dark blue pane and, looking through the centre, remarked to his companion, I see no sunshine, the day is dreary and the clouds cast gloomy shadows upon the horizon.

"Each one returned to relate their impressions of the weather, and the prince wondered at the different visions, unable to understand the reason."

There, concluded the Shogun, that is what happens to people who do not practise moderation.

Those, who see things through the medium of enthusiasm refuse to recognize that they could be deprived of brilliancy and beauty.

The others, those who look upon things from a pessimistic standpoint, never find anything in them save pretexts for pouring out to their hearers tales of woe and misery.

All find themselves deceptively allured; some rush toward

illusion, others do not wish to admit the positive chances for success, and both lacking moderation, they start from a basis of false premises from which they draw deplorable conclusions, thus defeating future success.

The spirit of penetration, according to the old Nippon philosopher, is not always a natural gift. "It is," said he, "a quality which certain people possess in a very high degree but which in spite this fact should be strengthened by will and discipline.

"One can easily acquire this faculty by endeavoring to foresee the solution of contemporary events; or at least try to explain the hidden reasons which have produced them.

"Great effects are produced, many times, from seemingly unimportant causes, and it is, above all, to the significant details that the spirit of penetration should give unceasing and undivided attention.

"Everything around us can serve as a subject for careful study; political events, incidents which interest family or friends, all may serve as just so many themes for earnest reflection.

"It is always preferable to confine this analysis to subjects in which we have no personal interest; thus we shall accustom ourselves to judge of people and things dispassionately and impersonally. This is the quality of mind necessary to the perfect development of penetration.

"If, for any reason, passion should create confusion of ideas, clearness of understanding would be seriously compromised and firmness of judgement, by deteriorating, would cast aside the manifestation of common sense.

"The spirit consistency is perhaps more difficult to

conquer, for it is a combination of many of the qualities previously mentioned.

"Its inspiration is drawn from the reasoning faculty, it cannot exist without moderation and implies a certain amount of penetration, because it must act under the authority of conviction.

"If you strike long enough in the same place on the thickest piece of iron, in time it will become as thin as the most delicate kakemono [a picture which hangs in Japanese homes].

"It is impossible to define the spirit of consistency more accurately.

"It is closely related to perseverance, but can not be confounded with it, because the attributes of consistency have their origin in logic and reason which does not produce one act alone but a series of acts sometimes dependent, always inferred.

"The spirit of consistency banishes all thought derogatory to the subject in question; it is the complete investiture of sentiments, all converging toward a unique purpose."

This purpose can be of very great importance and the means of attainment multiform, but the dominant idea will always direct the continuous achievements; under their different manifestations—and these at times contradictory—they will never be other than the emanation of a direct thought, whose superior authority is closely united to the final success.

Wisdom, continued the philosopher, should be mentioned here only as the forerunner which permits us to analyse experience.

COMMON SENSE: WHAT IS IT?

It is from this never-ending lesson which life teaches us that the wisdom of old age is learned.

But is it really necessary to reach the point of decrepitude, in order to profit by an experience, actually useless at that time, as is always a posthumous conquest.

"Is it not much better to compel its attainment when the hair is black and the heart capable of hope?

"Why give to old age alone the privileges of wisdom and experience? "It is high time to combat so profound an error.

"Is it not a cruel irony which renders such a gift useless?

"Of what benefit is wisdom resulting from experience if it cannot preserve us from the unfortunate seduction of youth?

"Why should its beauty be unveiled only to those who can no longer profit by it?" This is the opinion of Yoritomo, who says:

"What would be thought of one who prided himself on possessing bracelets when he had lost his two arms in war?

"It is, therefore, necessary, not only to encourage young people to profit by lessons of wisdom and experience, but, still further, to indicate to them how they can accomplish the result of these lessons.

"It is certain that he who can recall a long life ought to understand better than the young man all the pitfalls with which it is strewn.

"But does he always judge of it without bias or prejudice?

"Does he not find acceptable pretexts for excusing his past faults and does he not exaggerate the rewards for excellence, which have accorded him advantages, due at times to chance or to the force of circumstances?

"Finally, the old man can not judge of the sentiments

which he held at twenty years of age, unless it be by the aid of reminiscences, more or less fleeting, and an infinitely attenuated intensity of representation.

"Emotive perception being very much weakened, the integrity of memory must be less exact.

"Then, in the recession of years, some details, which were at times factors of the initial idea, are less vivid, thus weakening the power of reason which was the excuse, the pretext, or the origin of the act.

"This is why, although we may honour the wisdom of the aged, it is well to acquire it at a time when we may use it as a precious aid.

"To those who insist that nothing is equivalent to personal experience, we shall renew our argument, begging them to meditate on the preceding lines, drawing their attention to the fact that a just opinion can only be formed when personal sentiment is excluded from the discussion.

"Is it, then, necessary to have experienced pain in order to prevent or cure it?

"The majority of physicians have never been killed by the disease they treat. "Does this fact prevent them from combatting disease victoriously?

"And since we are speaking of common sense we shall not hesitate to invoke it in this instance, and all will agree that it should dictate our reply.

"Then why could we not do for the soul that which can be done for the body?

"It is first from books, then from the lessons of life that physicians learn the principles underlying their knowledge of disease and its healing remedies.

COMMON SENSE: WHAT IS IT?

"Is it absolutely indispensable for us to poison ourselves in order to know that such and such a plant is harmful and that another contains the healing substance which destroys the effects of the poison?

"We may all possess wisdom if we are willing to be persuaded that the experience of others is as useful as our own."

The events which multiply about us, Yoritomo says, ought to be, for each master, an opportunity for awakening in the soul of his disciples a perfect reasoning power, starting from the inception of the premises to arrive at the conclusions of all arguments.

From the repetition of events, from their correlation, from their equivalence, from their parallelism, knowledge will be derived and will be productive of good results, in proportion as egotistical sentiment is eliminated from them; and slowly, with the wisdom acquired by experience, common sense will manifest itself tranquil and redoubtable, working always for the accomplishment of good as does everything which is the emblem of strength and peace.

2

THE FIGHT AGAINST ILLUSION

Common Sense such as we have just described it, according to Yoritomo, is the absolute antithesis of dreamy imagination, it is the sworn enemy of illusion, against which it struggles from the moment of contact.

Common sense is solid, illusion is yielding, also illusion never issues victorious from a combat with it; during a struggle illusion endeavors vainly to display its subterfuges and cunning; illusions disappear one by one, crusht by the powerful arms of their terrible adversary—common sense.

"The worship of illusion," says Yoritomo, "presents certain dangers to the integrity of judgement, which, under such influence, falsifies the comparative faculty, and sways decision to the side of neutrality.

"This kind of mental half-sleep is extremely detrimental to manifestations of reason, because this torpor excludes it from imaginary conceptions.

"Little by little the lethargy caused by this intellectual paralysis produces the effect of fluidic contagion over all our faculties.

"Energy, which ought to be the principle factor in our resolutions, becomes feeble and powerless at the point where we no longer care to feel its influence.

"The sentiment of effort exists no longer, since we are pleased to resolve all difficulties without it.

"In this inconstant state of mind, common sense, after wandering a moment withdraws itself, and we find that we are delivered over to all the perils of imagination.

"Nothing that we see thus confusedly is found on the plane which belongs to common sense; the ideas, associated by a capricious tie, bind and unbind themselves, without imposing the necessity of a solution.

"The man who allows himself to be influenced by vague dreams," adds the Shogun, "must, if he does not react powerfully, bid farewell to common sense and reason; for he will experience so great a charm in forgetting, even for one moment, the reality of life, that he will seek to prolong this blest moment.

"He will renounce logic, whose conclusions are, at times, opposed to his desires, and he will plunge himself into that false delight of awakened dreams, or, as some say, day-dreams.

"Those who defend this artificial conception of happiness, like to compare people of common sense to heavy infantry soldiers, who march along through stony roads, while they depict themselves as pleasant bird-fanciers, giving flight to the fantastic bearers of wings.

"But they do not take into account the fact that the birds, for whom they open the cage, fly away without the intention of returning, leaving them thus deceived and deprived of the birds, while the rough infantry soldiers, after many hardships, reach the desired end which they had proposed to attain, thus realizing the joys of conquest.

"There they find the rest and security, which the possessors of fugitive birds will never know.

"Those who cultivate common sense will always ignore the collapses which follow the disappearance of illusions.

"How many men have suffered thus uselessly!

"And what is more stupid than a sorrow, voluntarily imposed, when it can not be productive of any good?

"Men can not be too strongly warned against the tendency of embellishing everything that concerns the heart-life, and this is the inclination of most people.

"The causes of this propensity are many and the need for that which astounds is not the only cause to be mentioned.

"Indolence is never a stranger to illusion.

"It is so delightful to foresee a solution which conforms to our desires!

"For certain natures, stained with moral atrophy, it is far sweeter to hope for that which will be produced without pain.

"One begins by accelerating this achievement, so earnestly desired, by using all the willpower, and one becomes accustomed progressively to regard desires as a reality, and, aided by indolence, man discounts in advance an easy success.

"False enthusiasm, or rather enthusiasm without deliberate reflection, always enters into these illusions, which are accompanied by persuasion and never combated by common sense.

"Vanity is never foreign to these false ideas, which are always of a nature to flatter one's amour propre.

"We love to rejoice beforehand in the triumph which

we believe will win and, aided by mental frivolity, we do not wish to admit that success can be doubted.

"The dislike of making an effort, however, would quickly conceal, with its languishing voice, the wise words of common sense, if we would listen momentarily to them.

"And, lastly, it is necessary to consider credulity, to which, in our opinion, is accorded a place infinitely more honourable than it deserves."

And now the sage, Yoritomo, establishes the argument which, by the aid of common sense, characterized these opinions.

According to him, "It does not belong to new and vibrating souls, as many would have us believe.

"When credulity does not proceed from inveterate stupidity, it is always the result of apathy and weakness.

"Unhappiness and misfortune attend those who are voluntarily feeble.

"Their defect deprived them of the joy derived from happy efforts. They will be the prey of duplicity and untruth.

"They are the vanquished in life, and scarcely deserve the pity of the conqueror; for their defeat lacks grandeur, since it has never been aurioled by the majestic strength of conflict."

Following this, the Shogun speaks to us of those whom he calls the ardent seekers after illusion.

One evening he related the following story: "Some men started off for an island, which they perceived in the distance.

"It looked like a large, detached red spot, amid the flaming rays of the setting sun, and the men told of a thousand wonders about this unknown land, as yet untrodden by the foot of man.

"The first days of the journey were delightful. The oars lay in the bottom of the boat untouched, and they just allowed themselves to drift with the tide. They disembarked, singing to the murmur of the waters, and gathered the fruits growing on the shores, to appease their hunger.

"But the stream, which was bearing them onward, did not retain long its limpidity and repose; the eddies soon entrapped the tiny bark and dragged the men overboard.

"Some, looking backward, were frightened at the thought of ascending the river, which had become so tempestuous.

"Escaping the wreckage of the boat as best they could, they entrusted themselves again to the fury of the waters.

"They had to suffer from cold and hunger, for they were far from shore, and as, in their imagination, the island was very near, they had neglected to furnish themselves with the necessities of life.

"At last, after the fatigues which forethought would have prevented, they found themselves one evening, at sundown, at the base of a great rock, bathed in the rosy light of the departing sun.

"This, then, was the island of their dreams.

"Tired out and exhausted from lack of food, they had only the strength to lie down upon the inhospitable rock, there to die!

"The disappearance of the illusion, having destroyed their courage and having struck them with the sword of despair, the rock of reality had proved destructive of their bodies and souls.

"The moral of this story easily unfolds itself.

"If the seekers after illusions had admitted common sense

THE FIGHT AGAINST ILLUSION

to their deliberations, they would certainly have learned to know the nature of the enchanted isle, and they would have taken good care not to start out on their journey which must terminate by such a deception.

"Would they not have taken the necessary precaution to prevent all the delays attendant upon travels of adventure, and would they have entrusted their lives to so frail a skiff, if they had acquired common sense?"

We must conclude, with Yoritomo, that illusion could often be transformed into happy reality if it were better understood, and if, instead of looking upon it through the dreams of our imagination, we applied ourselves to the task of eliminating the fluid vapours which envelop it, that we might clothe it anew with the garment of common sense.

Many enterprises have been considered as illusions because we have neglected to awaken the possibilities which lay dormant within them.

The initial thought, extravagant as it may appear, brings with it, at times, facilities of realization that a judgement dictated by common sense can alone make us appreciate.

He who knows how to keep a strict watch over himself will be able to escape the causes of disillusion, which lead us through fatal paths of error, to the brink of despair.

"That which is above all to be shunned," said the philosopher, "is the encroachment of discouragement, the result of repeated failures.

"Rare are those who wish to admit their mistakes.

"In the structure of the mind, inaccuracy brings a partial deviation from the truth, and it does not take long for this slight error to generalize itself, if not corrected by its natural reformer—common sense.

"But how many, among those who suffer from these unhappy illusions, are apt to recognize them as such?

"It would, however, be a precious thing for us to admit the causes which have led us to such a sorry result, by never permitting them to occur again.

"This would be the only way for the victims of illusion to preserve the life of that element of success and happiness known as hope.

"Because of seeing so often the good destroyed, we wish to believe no more in it as inherent in our being, and rather than suffer repeatedly from its disappearance, we prefer to smother it before perfect development.

"The greater number of skeptics are only the unavowed lovers of illusion; their desires, never being those capable of realization, they have lost the habit of hoping for a favourable termination of any sentiment.

"The lack of common sense does not allow them to understand the folly of their enterprise, and rather than seek the causes of their habitual failures, they prefer to attack God and man, both of whom they hold responsible for all their unhappiness.

"They are willingly ironical, easily become pessimists, and villify life, without desiring to perceive that it reserved as many smiles for them as the happy people whom they envy.

"All these causes of disappointment can only be attributed to the lack of equilibrium of the reasoning power and, above all, to the absence of common sense, hence we cannot judge of relative values.

"To give a definite course to the plans which we form

THE FIGHT AGAINST ILLUSION

is to prepare the happy termination of them.

"This is also the way to banish seductive illusion, the devourer of beautiful ambitions and youthful aspirations."

And, with his habitual sense of the practical in life, Yoritomo adds the following:

"There are, however, some imaginations which can not be controlled by the power of reasoning, and which, in spite of everything, escape toward the unlimited horizons of the dream.

"It would be in vain to think of shutting them up in the narrow prison walls of strict reason; they would die wishing to attempt an escape.

"To these we can prescribe the dream under its most august form, that of science.

"Each inventor has pursued an illusion, but those whose names have lived to reach our recognition, have caught a glimpse of the vertiginous course they were following, and no longer have allowed themselves to get too far away from their base—science.

"Yes, illusion can be beautiful, on condition that it is not constantly debilitated.

"To make it beautiful we must be its master, then we may attempt its conquest.

"It is thus that all great men act; before adopting an illusion, as truth, they have assured themselves of the means by the aid of which they were permitted first to hope for its transformation and afterward be certain of their power to discipline it.

"Illusion then changes its name and becomes the Ideal.

"Instead of remaining an inaccessible myth, it is

transformed into an entity for the creation of good.

"It is no longer the effort to conquer the impossible, which endeavor saps our vital forces; it is a contingency which study and common sense strip of all aleatory principles, in order to give a form which becomes more tangible and more definite every day.

"We have nothing more to do with sterile efforts toward gaining an object which fades from view and disappears as one approaches it.

"It is no longer the painful reaching out after an object always growing more in-distinct as we draw near it.

"It is through conscious and unremitting effort that we attain the happy expression of successful endeavor and realize the best in life, for slow ascension in winning this best leaves no room for satiety in this noble strife.

"We must pity those who live for an illusion as well as those whose imagination has not known how to create an ideal, whose beauty illumines their efforts.

"It is the triumph of common sense to accomplish this transformation and to banish empty reveries, replacing them by creating a desire for the best, which each one can satisfy—without destroying it.

"The day when this purpose is accomplished, illusion, definitely conquered, will cease to haunt the mind of those whom common sense has illumined; vagaries will make place for reason, and terrible disillusion will follow its chief (whose qualities never rise above mediocrity) into his retreat, and allow the flower of hope to blossom in the souls already filled with peace—that quality which is born of reason and common sense."

3

THE DEVELOPMENT OF THE REASONING POWER

When reading certain passages in the manuscripts of Yoritomo, one is forcibly reminded of the familiar phrase: "Nothing is definitely finished among men, for each thing stops only to begin again."

He says, "That many centuries before the great minds constructed altars to the goddess of Reason, they were in search of a divinity to replace the one they had just destroyed.

"If it were proposed to me to build temples which would synthesize my devotion with certain sentiments, my desire would be that those dedicated to the Will and to Reason should dominate all others, for then they would be under the protection of powers for good."

In a few pages further on he insists again and again upon the necessity of developing the worship of reason.

"Reasoning," he continues, "is a divinity, around which gravitate a whole world of gods, important but inferior to it.

"Among this people of these idols, so justly revered, there

is one god which occupies a place apart from the others.

"This god is Common Sense, which gave birth to Reason, and has always been its faithful companion.

"It is, in reality, the controlling force exercising its power to guard reason against the predominating character and nefarious tendencies created by self-interest.

"Common sense compels reason to admit principles whose justice it has already recognized, and, at the same time, incites reason to reject those whose absurdity it has demonstrated.

"Common sense allies itself with reason, in order to make that selection of ideas which personal interest can either set aside entirely or modify by illogical inference.

"Reason obeys certain laws, all of which can be united in one sentiment—common sense."

This statement could be illustrated symbolically by comparing its truth to a fan, whose blades converge toward a central point where they remain fixt.

Applying the precept to the picture, the old Shogun gives the design which we are faithfully copying.

"In this ideal fan," explains Yoritomo, "not only the true reproduction of the qualities directing the progress of knowledge must be perceived, but the symbol of their development must be traced.

"All of these qualities are born of common sense, to which they are closely allied, unfolding and disclosing a luminous radiance.

"Although each one may have its autonomy, they never separate, and, even as a fan from which one blade has disappeared can only remain an imperfect object little to be desired, even so, the symbolic fan of reasoning, when it does not unite all the required qualities, becomes a mutilated power, which can only betray the destiny originally attributed to it.

"Consequently, starting from common sense as the central point of reasoning, we find, first, perception.

"This is the action by which exterior things are brought near to us.

"Perception is essentially visual and auditory, although it influences all our senses. "For example, the fact of tasting a fruit is a perception.

"The seeing of a landscape is equally one. "The hearing of a song is also a perception.

"In a word, everything which presents itself to us, coming in contact with one of our senses, is a perception; otherwise, the inception of an idea.

"This is the first degree of reasoning.

"Immediately following is memory, without which nothing could be proved.

"It is memory, which, by renewing the motive power of reason, allows us to judge of the proportion of things, grasped by the senses in the present as related to those which come to us from the past.

"Without memory it would be impossible to make a mental comparison.

"It would be most difficult to determine the true nature of an event, announced by perception, if an analogous sensation, previously experienced, had not just permitted us to classify it by close examination or by differentiating it.

"Memory is a partial resurrection of a past life, whose

reconstruction has just permitted us to attribute a true value to the phases of existence.

"It is in preserving the memory of things that we are called upon to compare them and then to judge of them.

"Thought is produced immediately after perception, and the recollection, very often automatic, that it creates within us.

"It is the inception of the idea which it engenders by a series of results.

"Thought permits the mind to exercise its judgement without allowing itself to be influenced by the greatness or humility of the idea.

"By virtue of corresponding recollections, it will associate the present perception with the past representations, and will take an extension, more or less pronounced, according to the degree of intellectuality of the thinker, and according to the importance of the object of its reflections.

"But rarely does the idea present itself alone.

"One thought almost always produces the manifestation of similar thoughts, which group themselves around the first idea as birds of the same race direct their flight toward the same country.

"Thought is the manifestation of the intellectual life; it palpitates in the brain of men as does the heart in the breast.

"It is thought which distinguishes men from animals, who have only instinct to guide them.

"It can be admitted, however, that this instinct is a kind of obscure thought for these inferior beings, from which reflection is eliminated, or, at least, reveals itself only as a vassal of material appetite.

"But with creatures who have intelligence, thought is a superior faculty, which aids the soul to free itself from the bondage of vulgar and limited impressions.

"When perception, memory, and thought unite to form judgement, activity of mind will become necessary, in order to accelerate the production of ideas in extending the field of imagination.

"Moral inertia is the most deplorable of all defects; it retards intellectual growth and hinders the development of personality.

"It is, in this understanding, the enemy of common sense, for it will admit voluntarily a reasoning power, existing per se, rather than make the necessary effort which will set free the truth and constitute an individual opinion.

"Vulgarity is, then, almost always the sign of mental sloth.

"It is not infrequent to see a mind of real capacity fall into error, where an intelligence of mediocre caliber asserts its efficiency. Indifference is the most serious obstacle to the attainment of judgement.

"Common sense demands a keen alertness of understanding, placed at the disposal of a reflection which appears at times slow of action, but which is long in being manifested only because of the desire to surround itself by all the guaranties of truth concerning the object in question.

"The fifth blade of the fan is the quality of deduction— the most solid basis for the judgements which are formed by common sense.

"By deduction we are able to solve all relative questions with perfect accuracy.

"It is by abstracting reckless contingencies, and by relying only upon the relativeness of facts, that we can succeed in discovering the truth that there are too many representations as to these facts.

"Deduction is the great support of mental weakness. It helps in discerning proportions, possibilities, even as it helps in skilfully avoiding the fear of error."

We shall have occasion to speak more at length of deduction, for Yoritomo devotes many pages to it. We shall, then, defer to a future chapter the interesting developments that he discloses on this subject, and we shall continue to study the fan of common sense with him.

"Foresight," he continues, "is rightly looked upon as one of the indispensable elements in cultivating common sense.

"The faculty of foresight always accompanies common sense, in order to strengthen its qualities of skill and observation.

"One must not confound, as many people are tempted to do, foresight and conjecture.

"The first consists in taking great care to prevent the repetition of unhappy facts which have already existed.

"Foresight will exert an influence on future events by establishing an analogy between them and the actual incidents which, of necessity, will lead to the adoption or rejection of present projects.

"It is to be observed that all these faculties are subordinate, one to the other, and, in proportion to the unfolding of the fan, we can prove that all the blades previously mentioned have concurred in the formation of the blade of which we are now speaking.

"In order to foresee disasters it is necessary that the

THE DEVELOPMENT OF THE REASONING POWER

perception—visual or auditory—of said disasters should already have imprest us.

"We have kept intact the memory of them, since it is reconstructed emotion which guides our thoughts.

"These same thoughts, in extending themselves, form groups of thoughts harmonious in character, all relative to the one, which is the object of the debate.

"Our mind becomes more active in recalling the incidents, the remembrance of which marks the time which has elapsed between the old perception and the present state of mental absorption.

"The faculty of deduction, which is born of these different mental conflicts, permits me to foresee that circumstances of the same nature will lead to others similar to those we have already mentioned.

"We have merely sketched rapidly the scale of sensations which follow each other, in order to reach the explanation of how foresight is formed, this faculty of which we are now speaking.

"By assimilating these present facts with those of the past, we are permitted to draw a conclusion, relating to the same group of results, because of the conformity of those past facts to the present questions.

"Foresight is passive; between it and precaution there is the same difference as between theory and practise.

"Precaution is preeminently active, and it marks its first appearance by means of foresight, but does not stop in this effort until it has rendered foresight productive.

"It is well to foresee, but it is precious to preclude.

"The second part of the act of precaution can, however,

only be accomplished after having permitted the brain to register the thoughts which determine the first part of this act."

In order to understand this very subtle difference, but very important one, which classifies these two sentiments, the old sage gives us the following example:

"Let us suppose," he says, "that, on a beautiful day in spring, a man starts out for an excursion which will last until the dawn of the following day.

"If he has common sense, he will say to himself that the sun will not be shining at the time of his return, that the nights of spring are cold, and that this one will be no exception to the rule.

"This is foresight.

"If common sense, with all its consequences, takes possession of him, it will increase his power of reasoning. He will think that, in order to avoid suffering from the change of temperature, it would be well to cover himself with a cloak.

"And, even tho the sun shone, he would not hesitate to furnish himself with this accessory, which in fact will render him the greatest service.

"This is precaution.

"This quality is indispensable to the formation of the reasoning power; for, in addition to the necessity of foreseeing certain results, it permits also of directing their course, if it be impossible to exempt them completely.

"Reasoning is the art of developing, to the highest degree, the suppositions resulting from deduction.

"One is usually mistaken as to the exact meaning of the

words 'to reason,' and people seldom attach the importance to them which they should.

"One is apt to think that the gift of reasoning is bestowed upon every one.

"Perhaps; but to reason, following the principles of justice and truth, is an operation which can only be performed by minds endowed with common sense.

"In order to arrive at this result, it is essential to impress upon oneself the value of the words, 'to deduct accurately,' after having produced the radiation of thoughts which depend upon the object in question, and to foresee the consequences of the facts that a resolution could determine.

"Above all, to avoid contentment with the approximate, which conceals many pitfalls under false appearances.

"Without permitting oneself to express useless trivialities, not to neglect to become impregnated with those axioms which have been rightfully baptized, 'wisdom of nations.'

"They are generally based on a secular observation, and are the product of many generations.

"It would be puerile to attach vital importance to them, but one would surely regret having entirely scorned their counsel.

"Too much erudition is at times detrimental to reason, based on common sense. Although fully appreciating science, and devoting serious study to it, one would do well to introduce the human element into his knowledge.

"There are some essential truths which modify daily life without, for this reason, lessening their importance.

"Some of them are of premature development; others are of miniature growth.

"To reason without offending common sense, it is, therefore, indispensable to consider time, place, environment, and all the contingencies which could arise to undermine the importance of reasoning."

After having reviewed all these phases, we shall then extend, in accord with Yoritomo, the last blade of this rudimentary fan, and we shall find judgement.

"This one is the index to that quality of mind called conviction.

"This mental operation consists in drawing together many ideas that their relative characteristics may be determined.

"This operation takes the place contiguous to reasoning, of which it is the result.

"Judgement determines its character after having registered the reasons which ought to indicate its position; it deducts the conclusions imposed by the explanatory principle, and classifies the idea by submitting it to the valuation placed upon it by judgement.

"All judgement is either affirmative or negative. "It can never be vascillating nor neutral.

"In this last case it will assume the title of opinion, and will attribute to itself the definite qualities which characterize judgement.

"It is, however, at times subjected to certain conditions, where the principles on which it is based are not sufficiently defined, and, therefore, becomes susceptible to a change, either of form or of nature.

"It is possible, without violating the laws of common sense, to establish a judgement whose terms will be modified by the mutation of causes.

"But common sense demands that these different influences should be foreseen, and that these eventualities should be mentioned when pronouncing the judgement."

We have reached the last blade of the symbolic fan, described by the philosopher, for many secondary qualities may be placed between the principle blades.

But faithful to his explanatory method, he wished to indicate to us the broad lines first, and also to state the indispensable faculties constituting common sense, by teaching us their progression and development.

He desired to demonstrate to us also how much all these qualities would be lessened in value if they were not united and bound together in the order in which they ought to manifest themselves.

"We have all possest," said he, "some fans whose point of reunion was destroyed in part or altogether lost.

"What becomes of it, then?

"During a certain length of time, always rather short, the blades, after having remained bound together by the thread which holds them, separate, when it is severed because of the lack of harmony and of equilibrium at their base.

"Very soon, one blade among them detaches itself, and the mutilated fan takes its place in the cemetery where sleep those things deteriorated because of old age or disuse.

"It is the same with the qualities which we have just enumerated. As long as they remain attached to their central point, which is common sense, they stand erect, beautiful and strong, concurring in the fertilization of our minds, and in creating peace in our lives.

"But if the point of contact ceases to maintain them, to

bind them together, to for-bid their separating, we shall soon see them fall apart after having escaped from the temporary protection of the secondary qualities.

"For a while we seek to evoke them; but recognizing the ruse existing in their commands, we shall soon be the first to abandon them, in order to harmonize our favours with the deceptive mirage of the illusions; at least, if we do not allow ourselves to be tempted by fallacious arguments of vanity.

"In the one as in the other case, we shall become, then, the prey of error and ignorance, for common sense is the intelligence of truth."

4

COMMON SENSE AND IMPULSE

Impulsive people are those who allow themselves to be guided by their initial impressions and make resolutions or commit acts tinder the domination of a special consciousness into which perception has plunged them.

Impulse is a form of cerebral activity which, forces us to make a movement before the mind is able to decide upon it by means of reflection or reasoning. The Shogun deals with it at length and defines it thus:

"Impulse is an almost direct contact between perception and result.

"Memory, thought, deduction, and, above all, reason are absolutely excluded from these acts, which are never inspired by intellectuality.

"The impression received by the brain is immediately transmuted into an act, similar to those acts which depend entirely on automatic memory.

"It is certain in making a series of movements, which compose the act of walking upstairs or the action of walking from one place to another, we do not think of analysing our efforts and this act of walking almost limits itself to an organic function, so little does thought enter into its composition.

"In the case of repeated impulses, it can be absolutely affirmed that substance is the antecedent and postulate of the essence of being.

"Substance comprises all corporal materialities: instinctive needs, irrational movements, in a word, all actions where common sense is not a factor.

"Essence is that imponderable part of being which includes the soul, the mind, the intelligence, in fact the entire mentality.

"It is this last element of our being which poetizes our thoughts, classifies them, and leads us to common sense, by means of reasoning and judgement.

"He who, having received an injury from his superior, replies to it at once by corresponding affront, is absolutely sure to become the victim of his impulses.

"It is only when his act is consummated, that he will think of the consequences which it can entail; the loss of his employment first, then corporal punishment, in severity according to the gravity of the offense; lastly, misery, perhaps the result of forced inactivity.

"On the contrary, the man endowed with common sense will reflect in a flash, by recalling all the different phases which we have described. His intelligence, being appealed to, will represent to him the consequences of a violent action.

"He will find, in common sense, the strength not to respond to an injury at once; but will not forego the right, however, of avenging himself under the guise of a satisfaction which will be all the more easily accorded to him as his moderation will not fail to make an impression in his favour."

"There is, between common sense and impulse," says Yoritomo, "the difference that one would find between two coats, one of which was bought ready-made, while the other, after being cut according to the proportions of the one who is to wear it, was sewed by a workman to whom all the resources of his art are known."

If impulses adopt the same character for every one, common sense adapts itself to the mind, to the sensitiveness, to the worth of him who practises it; it is a garment which is adjusted to the proportions of its owner, and, according to his taste, is elaborate or simple.

Certain people have a tendency to confound intuition and impulse.

These two things, really very different in essence, are only related by spontaneity of thought which gives them birth.

But whereas intuition, a sensation altogether moral, concisely stated, is composed of mental speculations, impulses always resolve themselves into acts and resolutions to act.

Intuition is a sort of obscure revelation, which reason controls only after its formation.

Impulse never engages common sense in the achievements which it realizes. It never decides upon them in advance, and almost always engenders regrets.

It is the result of a defeat in self-control, which willpower and the power of reasoning alone can correct.

Intuition is less spontaneous than impulse.

It is a very brief mental operation, but, nevertheless, very real, which, very indistinctly, touches lightly all the phases of reasoning, in order to reach a conclusion so rapidly that he who conceives it has difficulty in making the transformations of the initial thought intelligible.

It is none the less true that intuition is always inspired by a predicted reflection, but, in spite of this fact, an existing reflection.

Impulse, on the contrary, only admits instinct as its source of existence.

It is the avowed enemy of common sense, which counsels the escape from exterior insinuations that one may concentrate, in order to listen to the voice which dictates to us the abstinence from doing anything until after making a complete analysis of the cause which agitates us.

Some philosophers have sought to rank inspiration under the flag of impulse, which they thought to defend; yes, even to recover esteem under this new form.

"We should know how to stand on guard," says Yoritomo, "against this fatal error."

"Inspiration," says he, "is rarely immobilized under the traits which characterized its first appearance.

"Before expressing itself in a work of art or of utility, it was the embryo of that which it must afterward personify.

"The ancients when relating that a certain divinity sprang, fully armed, from the head of a god, accredited this belief to instantaneous creation.

"If musicians, painters, poets, and inventors want to be sincere, they will agree that, between the thought which they qualify as inspiration, and its tangible realization, a ladder of transformations has been constructed, and that it is only by progressive steps that they have attained what seemed to them the nearest to perfection."

Impulse, then, is only distantly related to inspiration and intuition.

Let us add that these gifts are very often only the fruit of an unconscious mental effort, and that, most of the time, the thoughts, which in good faith one accepts as inspiration or intuition, are only nameless reminiscences, whose apparition coincides with an emotional state of being, which existed at the time of the first perception.

There, again, the presence of reasoning is visible, and also the presence of common sense, which tries to convert into a work of lasting results those impressions which would probably remain unproductive without the aid of these two faculties.

Impulses are, most of the time, the vassals of material sensations.

Definite reasoning and impartial judgement, inspired by common sense, are rarely the possession of a sick man.

Sufferings, in exposing him to melancholy, make him see things in a defective light; the effort of thinking fatigues his weak brain, and the fear of a resolution which would force him to get out of his inactivity has enormous influence upon the deductions which dictate his judgement.

Before discussing the advantages of conflict, he will instinctively resign himself to inertia.

If, on the contrary, his temperament disposes him to anger, he will compromise an undertaking by a spontaneous violence, which patience and reflection would otherwise have made successful. It is possible also that a valiant soul is unable to obey a weak body, and that instinct, awakened by fear, leads one on to the impulsive desires of activity.

Inadequate food or excessive nourishment can produce impulses of a different nature, but these differences are wholly and completely distinct as to character.

The most evident danger of impulses lies in the scattering of mental forces, which, being too frequently called upon, use themselves up without benefiting either reason or common sense.

The habit of indulging in movements dictated only by instinct, in suppressing all the phases of judgement leaves infinitely more latitude to caprice, which exists at the expense of solid judgement.

Perception, being related to that which interests our passions, by getting in direct contact with the action which should simply be derived from a deduction, inspired by common sense, multiplies the unreflected manifestations and produces waste of the forces, which should be concentrated on a central point, after having passed through all the phases of which we have spoken.

In addition, the permanency of resolutions is unknown to impulsive people.

Their tendency, by leading them on toward instantaneous solutions, allows them to ignore the benefits of consistency.

"They are like unto a peasant," said the old Nippon, "who owned a field in the country of Tokio. Scarcely had he begun to sow a part of the field when, under the influence of an unhappy impulse, he plowed up the earth again in order to sow the ground with a new seed.

"If he heard any one speak of any special new method of cultivation, he only tried it for a short while, and then abandoned it, to try another way.

"He tried to cultivate rice; then, before the time for harvesting it, he became enthusiastic for the cultivation of chrysanthemums, which he abandoned very soon in order to plant trees, whose slow development incited him to change his nursery into a field of wheat.

"He died in misery, a victim of his having scorned the power of consistency and common sense."

Now Yoritomo, after having put us on our guard against impulses, shows us the way to conquer these causes of disorder.

"To control unguarded movements, which place us on a level with inferior beings. That is," said he "in making us dependent on one instinct alone. This is," said he, "to take the first step toward the will to think, which is one of the forms of common sense.

"In order to reach this point, the first resolution to make is to escape from the tyranny of the body, which tends to replace the intellectual element in impulsive people.

"When I was still under the instruction of my preceptor, Lang-Ho, I saw him cure a man who was affected with what he called 'The Malady of the First Impulse.'

"Whether it concerned good actions or reprehensible ones, this man always acted without the least reflection.

"To launch a new enterprise, which the most elementary common sense condemned, he gave the greater part of his fortune in a moment of enthusiasm.

"He allowed himself to commit acts of violence which taught him severe lessons.

"Finally, vexed beyond measure, dissatisfied with himself and others, he so brutally maltreated a high dignitary in a moment of violent anger that the latter sent for him that he might punish him. Learning of this, the man, crazy with rage, rushed out of his house in order to kill the prince with his own hand.

"It was in this paroxysm of passion that my master met him. Like all impulsive people, he was full of his subject, and, joining the perception of the insult to the judgement of it, which his instinct had immediately dictated to him, he did not conceal his murderous intentions.

"My master, by means of a strategy, succeeded in dissuading him from accomplishing his revenge that day. He persuaded him that the prince was absent and would only return to town upon the following day.

"The man believed him, and allowed himself to be taken to the house of Lang-Ho.

"But it was in vain that Lang-Ho unfolded all his most subtle arguments. Neither the fear of punishment, nor the hope of pardon, could conquer the obstinacy which can always be observed in impulsive people when their resolution has not accomplished its purpose.

"It was then that my master employed a ruse, whose fantastic character brings a smile, but which, however, demonstrates a profound knowledge of the human heart when acting under the influence of common sense.

"During the sleep of his guest, Lang-Ho took off his robe, replacing it by a garment made of two materials. One was golden yellow, the other a brilliant green. After attacks of terrible anger, in spite of the solicitation of his impulsive nature which incited him to go out, he did not dare to venture into the streets in such a costume.

"That which the most subtle arguments had been unable to accomplish, was obtained through fear of ridicule.

"Two days passed; his fury was changed into great mental exhaustion, because impulsive people can not withstand the contact with obstacles for any length of time.

"It was this moment which my master chose to undertake the cure, in which he was so vitally interested.

"With the most delicate art, he explained to the impulsive man all the chain of sentiments leading from perception to judgement.

"He caused common sense to intervene so happily that the man was permeated by it. My master kept him near by for several weeks, always using very simple arguments to combat the instinctive resolutions which were formulated in his brain many times a day.

"Common sense, thus solicited, was revealed to the impulsive one, and appeared like a peaceful counselor.

"The ridiculous and odious side of his resolution was represented to him with such truth that he embraced Lang-Ho, saying:

"'Now, Master, I can go away, and your mind can be at rest about me.

"'The arguments of common sense have liberated me from bondage in which my lack of reflection held me.

"'I return to my home, but, I beg of you, allow me to take away this ridiculous costume which was my savior.

"'I wish to hang it in my home, in the most conspicuous place, that, from the moment my nature incites me to obey the commands of impulse, I may be able to look at once upon this garment, and thus recall your teachings, which have brought sweetness and peace into my life.'"

All those who are inclined to act by instinct should follow this example, not by dressing up in a ridiculous robe half green and half yellow, but by placing obstacles in the way of the accomplishment of impulsive acts, which the dictates of common sense would not sanction.

"For those whose mind possess a certain delicacy," again says the old master, "these obstacles will be of a purely moral order, but for those who voluntarily allow themselves to be dominated by a diseased desire for action, obstacles should adopt a tangible form; the difficulty in conquering anything always makes impulsive people reflect a little.

"Under the immediate impression of the perception of an act they are ready for a struggle to the death; but this ardor is quickly extinguished, and inertia, in its turn, having become an impulse, makes them throw far away from them the object which determined the effort.

"In proportion as they encounter obstacles, which they have taken the precaution to raise, the encroachment of the impression will make itself less felt.

"The mere fact of having foreseen will become a matter for reflection for them.

"The feeling of the responsibilities will be roused in them, and they will understand how difficult it is to escape the consequences of impulsive acts."

Would one not say that these lines had been written yesterday?

More than ever our age of unrest makes us the prey of impulses, and to the majority of our contemporaries, the robe, half green and half yellow (by recalling to them the worship of common sense), will become a fetish, more precious than all the amulets with which superstition loves to adorn logic, or to incorporate fantastic outline in the classic setting of beautiful jewels.

5

THE DANGERS OF SENTIMENTALITY

The Shogun says: "There are sentimentalities of many kinds, some present less dangers than others, but from every point of view they are prejudicial to the acquisition and exercise of common sense. To cultivate sentiment over which the Will has no control is always to be regretted.

"Sentimentality is multiform.

"It presents itself, at times, under the aspect of an obscure appeal to sensuality and brings with it a passing desire of the heart and of the senses, which produces an artificial appreciation of the emotion felt.

"In this first case sentimentality is an unconscious manifestation of egotism, because, outside of that which provokes this outward manifestation, everything is alienated and becomes indistinct.

"The incidents of existence lose their true proportion, since everything becomes relative to the object because of our preoccupation.

"The impulse reigns supreme there when sentimentality establishes itself, and the desire of judgement, if it makes itself apparent, is quickly shunned, to the profit of illusory reasons, in which pure reason does not intervene.

"This sentimentality amalgamating the springs of egotism bereaves the soul's longing of all its greatness.

"The anxiety to attribute all our impressions to emotion is only a way of intensifying it for our personal satisfaction, at the expense of a sentiment far deeper and more serious, which never blossoms under the shadow of egotism and of frivolous sentimentality.

"Never will common sense have the chance to manifest itself in those who permit such ephemeral and enfeebling impressions to implant themselves in their souls.

"However they must be pitied because their artificial emotion often results in a sorrow which is not lessened by repetition, but whose manifestation is none the less prejudicial to the peace of their being.

"All those who do not harmonize common sense and the emotions of the heart become passive to the investiture of a sentimentality which does not wait to know if the object be worthy of them before it exists in consciousness.

"From this state of mind arise disillusions and their recurrence entails a defect in the conception.

"Men who are often deceived in allowing themselves to feel a sorrow which is only based on the longings of sentimentality become pessimists quickly and deny the existence of deep and enduring affection judged from its superior expression.

"This superior expression of sentiment is freed from all personality and such judgement which differentiates it from other sentiments.

"If we wished to appeal to common sense we should acknowledge, too often, that in the search for expansion we have only recognized the opportunity to satisfy the inclination which urges us to seek for pleasure.

"Sentiment reasons, and is capable of devotion. Sentimentality excludes reflective thought and ignores generosity.

"We are capable of sacrificing ourselves for sentiment.
"Sentimentality exacts the sacrifice of others.

"Therefore, profiting by the principles already developed, he who cultivates common sense will never fail to reason in the following manner:

"Opening the symbolic fan, he will encounter, after perfection, the memory which will suggest to him the recollections of personal and strange experiences and he will record this fact: abegation is rarely encountered.

"The inclination of our thoughts will suggest to us the difficulties there are in searching for it.

"Deduction will acquaint us with the temerity of this exaction, and precaution will attract our thoughts to the possibility of suffering which could proceed from disillusion.

"Following this, reasoning and judgement will intervene in order to hasten the conclusion formulated by common sense.

"It follows then that, abnegation being so rare, common sense indicates to me that it would be imprudent for me to allow my happiness to rest upon the existence of a thing so exceptional.

"For this reason this sentimental defect will find common sense armed against this eventuality.

THE DANGERS OF SENTIMENTALITY

"There is another form or sentimentality not less common.

"It is that which extends itself to all the circumstances of life and transforms true pity into a false sensibility, the exaggeration of which deteriorates the true value of things.

"Those who give publicity to this form of sentiment are agitated (or imagine themselves to be agitated) as profoundly on the most futile of pretexts as for the most important cause.

"They do not think to ask themselves if their ardor is merited; also every such experience, taking out of them something of their inner selves, leaves them enfeebled and stranded.

"Every excursion into the domain of sentimentality is particularly dangerous, for tourists always fail to carry with them the necessary coinage which one calls common sense."

After having put ourselves on guard against the surprizes of mental exaggeration, Yoritomo warns us of a kind of high respectable sentimentality which we possess, that is none the less censurable because under an exterior of the purest tenderness it conceals a profound egotism.

It concerns paternal love from which reasoning and common sense are excluded.

"Nothing" said he, "seems more noble than the love of parents for their children, and no sentiment is more august when it is comprehended in all its grandeur.

"But how many people are apt to distinguish it from an egotistical sentimentality.

"I have seen some mothers oppose the departure of their sons, preferring to oblige them to lead an obscure existence near to them, rather than impose upon themselves the sorrow of a separation.

"These women do not fail to condemn the action of others, who, filled with a sublime abnegation, allow their children to depart, hiding from them the tears which they shed, because they have the conviction of seeing them depart for the fortune and the happiness which they feel themselves unable to offer them.

"Which of these are worthy of admiration? Those who condemn their children to a life of mediocrity in order to obey an egotistical sentimentality, or those who, with despair in their hearts, renounce the joy of their presence, and think only of their own grief in order to build upon it the happiness of their dear ones.

"The common sense of this latter class inspiring in them this magnificent sentiment, and forcing them to set aside a sentimentality which is, in reality, only the caricature of sentiment, has permitted them to escape that special kind of egotism, which could be defined thus: The translation of a desire for personal contentment.

"Ought we then to blame others so strongly?

"It is necessary, above all, to teach them to reason about the ardor of their emotions, and only to follow them when they find that they are cleansed from all aspiration which is not a pledge of devotion."

Now the Shogun speaks to us with that subtlety of analysis which is characteristic and refers to a kind of sentimentality the most frequent and the least excusable.

"There are," he tells us, "a number of people who, without knowing that they offend common sense in a

THE DANGERS OF SENTIMENTALITY

most indefensible manner, invoke sentimentality in order to dispense with exercising the most vulgar pity, to the profit of their neighbor.

"A prince," he continues, "possest a large? tract of land which he had put under grain.

"For the harvest, a large number of peasants and labourers were employed and each one lived on the products of his labour.

"But a prolonged drought threatened the crop; so the prince's overseer dismissed most of the labourers, who failed to find employment in the parched country.

"Soon hunger threatened the inmates of the miserable dwellings, and sickness, its inseparable companion, did not fail to follow.

"Facing the conditions the prince left, and had it not been for two or three wealthy and charitable people the labourers would have starved to death.

"This pitiful condition was soon changed, abundance replaced famine, and the master returned to live in his domain.

"But amazement followed when he addresst his people as follows: Here I am, back among you, and I hope to remain here a long time; if I left you, it was because I have so great an affection for all my servants and because even the bare thought of seeing them suffer caused me unbearable sorrow.

"I am not among those who are sufficiently hard-hearted to be able to take care of sick and suffering people and to be a witness of their martyrdom. My pity is too keen to permit of my beholding this spectacle; this is why I had to leave to others, less sensitive, the burden of care which my too tender heart was unable to lavish on you."

And that which is more terrible is that this man believed what he said.

He did not understand the monstrous rent which he made in the robe of common sense, by declaring that he had committed the vilest act of cruelty due to excessive sensitiveness since it represented a murderous act of omission.

Examples of this form of sentimentality are more numerous than we think.

There exist people who cover their dogs with caresses, gorging them with dainties, and will take good care not to succor the needy.

Others faint away at sight of an accident and never think of giving aid to the wounded.

One may observe that for people exercising sentimentality at the expense of common sense, the greatest catastrophe in intensity, if it be far away from us, diminishes, while the merest incident, a little out of the ordinary, affects them in a most immoderate manner if it be produced in the circle of their acquaintances.

It is needless to add that, if it touches them directly, it becomes an unparalleled calamity; it seems that the rest of the world must be troubled by it.

This propensity toward pitying oneself unreasonably about little things which relate to one directly and this exaggerated development of a sterile sentimentality are almost always artificial, and the instinct of self-preservation very often aids in their extermination.

"Among my old disciples," pursues the Shogun, "I had a friend whose son was afflicted by this kind of sentimentality, the sight of blood made him faint and he was incapable of aiding any one whomsoever; that which he called his good heart, and which was only a form of egotistical sentimentality, prevented him from looking at the suffering of others.

"One day, a terrible earthquake destroyed his palace; he escaped, making his way through the ruins and roughly pushing aside the wounded who told about it afterward.

"I saw him some days after; instead of reproaching him severely for his conduct, I endeavored to make him see how false was his conception of pity, since, not only had he not fainted at the sight of those who, half-dead, were groaning, but he had found in the egotistical sentiment of self-preservation the strength to struggle against those who clung to him, beseeching him for help.

"I demonstrated to him the evident contradiction of his instinctive cruelty to the sentimentality that it pleased him to make public.

"I made an appeal to common sense, in order to prove to him the attitude which he had, until then, assumed, and I had the joy of seeing myself understood.

"My arguments appealed to his mentality, and always afterward, when he had the opportunity to bring puerile sentimentality and common sense face to face, he forced himself to appeal to that quality, which in revealing to him the artifice of the sentiment which animated him, cured him of false sensibility, which he had displayed up to that time."

Sentimentality is in reality only a conception of egotism, under the different forms which it adopts.

Yoritomo proves it to us again, in speaking of the weakness of certain teachers, who, under the pretext of avoiding trouble, allow their children to follow their defective inclinations.

"It is by an instinctive hatred of effort that parents forbid themselves to make their children cry when reprimanding them," said he.

"If the parents wish to be sincere to themselves, they will perceive that the sorrow in seeing their children's tears flow, plays a very small part in their preconceived idea of indulgence.

"It is in order to economize their own nervous energy or to avoid cleverly the trouble of continued teaching, that they hesitate to provoke these imaginary miseries, the manifestation of which is caused by the great weakness of the teachers.

"Common sense, nevertheless, ought to make them understand that it is preferable to allow the little ones to shed a few tears, which are quickly dried, rather than to tolerate a deplorable propensity for these habits which, later in life, will cause them real anxiety."

And the philosopher concludes:

"A very little reasoning could suffice to convince one of the dangers of sentimentality, if the persons who devote themselves entirely to it consented to reflect, by frankly agreeing to the true cause which produces it.

"They would discover in this false pity the desire not to disturb their own tranquility.

"They would also perceive that, in order to spare themselves a few unpleasant moments in the present they are preparing for themselves great sorrow for the future.

"In parental affection, as in friendship or in the emotions

THE DANGERS OF SENTIMENTALITY

of love, sentimentality is none other than an exaggerated amplification of the ego.

"If it be true that all our acts, even those most worthy of approbation, can react in our personality, at least it is necessary that we should be logical and that, in order to create for ourselves a partial happiness or to avoid a temporary annoyance, we should not prepare for ourselves an existence, outlined by deception and fruitless regrets.

"Sentimentality and its derivatives, puerile pity and false sensitiveness, can create illusion for those who do not practise the art of reasoning, but the friends of common sense do not hesitate to condemn them for it.

"In spite of the glitter in which it parades itself, sentimentality will never be anything but the dross of true sentiment."

6

THE UTILITY OF COMMON SENSE IN DAILY LIFE

As our philosopher explains, the influence of common sense is above all appreciation of daily events. "We have," he continues, "very rarely in life the opportunity of making grave decisions, but we are called upon daily to resolve unimportant problems, and we can only do it in a judicious way, if we are allowed to devote ourselves to certain kinds of investigation.

"This is what may be called to judge with discrimination, otherwise, with common sense.

"Without this faculty, it is in vain that our memory amasses the materials, which must serve us in the comparative examination of facts.

"And this examination can only be spoiled by decrepitude, if common sense did not succeed in dictating its conclusions to us.

"Thanks to this faculty, we possess this accuracy of mind which permits us to discern truth from falsehood.

THE UTILITY OF COMMON SENSE IN DAILY LIFE

"It is this power which aids us in distinguishing what we should consider as a duty, as a right, or as a thing conforming to equity, established by the laws of intelligence.

"Without common sense, we should be like an inexperienced gardener, who, for want of knowledge, would allow the trees to grow and would neglect the plants whose function is to nourish man.

"In order to conform to the habit of judging with common sense, one ought first to lay down the following principle:

"No fact can exist, unless there is a sufficient motive to determine its nature.

"It is when operating on the elements furnished us by common sense that we are able to discern the quality of the object of our attention.

"One day, a sage, whom people gladly consulted, was asked by what means he had learned to know so well the exact proportion of things, so that he never failed to attribute to them their real value.

"'Why' they added, 'can you foresee so exactly the evil and direct us to that which is right and just?'

"And the superstitious people added:

"'Are you not in communication with the spirits, which float in space, which come from the other world?

"Would you not be counselled by voices which we have not the power to hear, and do you not see things which are visible to you alone?'

"'You are right,' replied the saintly man, smiling:

"'I have indeed the power to hear and to see that which you do not perceive; but sorcery has no relation to the power which is attributed to me.

"If you wish, you will be able to possess it in your turn, for my means are not a secret.

"'I keep my eyes and ears open.'

"And as every one burst out laughing, believing it a joke, the sage began again:

"'But this is not all; after having seen and heard, I call to my aid all the qualities which constitute common sense and, thanks to this faculty, I draw my conclusions from my experience, from which enthusiasm, fancy, as well as personal interest are totally excluded.

"'This done, and my judgement being formulated in my thought, I adapt it to the circumstances, and especially to the material situation and to the mentality of those who consult me.'

"From these counsels," thinks the Shogun, "we must draw a precious lesson.

"It is true that an exigency, physical or moral, can determine, in different individuals, a very different resolution.

"According to the manner of life adopted, or the direction given to one's duties, different resolutions can be made without lacking common sense. It is indisputable that what represents social obligations does not demand the same conduct from the peasant as from the prince.

"We should outrage common sense in presenting a workman with a gorgeous robe suitable for great ceremonies, in which to do his work, but reason would be equally outraged if one put on a shabby costume to go to the palace of the Mikado."

The nature of resolutions inspired by common sense varies according to environment, the time, and the state of mind in which one is.

These conditions make of this quality a virtue really worth acquiring, for it is more difficult to conquer than many others and its effects are of infinite variety.

But as always, Yoritomo, after having signalled the danger, and indicated the remedy, gives us the manner of its application.

That which follows is marked by that simplicity of conception and facility of execution which render the doctrine of the Nippon philosopher absolutely efficacious.

Instead of losing himself by digressing from his subject and by placing himself on the summits of psychology, he remains with us, puts himself on the level of the most humble among us, and says to us all:

"The best way to use common sense in daily life consists in declaring one's honest intentions.

"What should I do if I were in the place of the person with whom I am discussing?

"I found myself one day on the slope of a hill named Yung-Tshi, and I remarked that the majority of the trees were stript of their foliage.

"The season seeming to me not sufficiently advanced for this condition of vegetation, I expressed my astonishment to a passer-by, who replied to me:

"'Alas! This occurs every year at the same time, and it is not well to cultivate trees on the height of Yung-Tshi, for the sun, being too hot, dries them up before the time when the foliage ought to fall.'

"A few days afterward my steps lead me on the opposite slope of the same hill.

"There the trees were covered with foliage, still green but uncommon, and their appearance indicated an unhealthy condition of growth.

"'Alas!' said a man who was working in the hedges to me, 'it is not well to cultivate trees on the height of Yung-Tshi, for the sun never shines there, and they can only acquire the vigour they would possess if they were planted in another country.'

"And, although recognizing the truth of these two opinions, so contradictory, I could not help thinking that they were the reproduction of those which men, deprived of common sense, express every day.

"The same hill produced a vegetation, affected in different ways, by reason of different causes; and the people, instead of taking into consideration how carelessly they had chosen the location of their plantation, preferred to attribute the defect to the site itself, rather than to their lack of precaution.

"Both of them were suffering from a hurtful exaggeration, but each one explained it in a way arbitrarily exclusive.

"He of the north made out that the sun never shone on the summit of Yung-Tshi, and the inhabitant of the south affirmed that the health-giving shade was unknown there."

This is why it is indispensable to the successful resolution of the thousand and one problems of daily life, both those whose sole importance is derived from their multiplicity and those whose seriousness justly demands our attention, to employ the very simple method which prescribes that we place ourselves mentally in the position and circumstances of the person with whom we are discussing.

THE UTILITY OF COMMON SENSE IN DAILY LIFE

If each one of the inhabitants of Yung-Tshi had followed this precept, instead of declaring that the hill never received the sun or that shade never fell upon it, they would each one have thought for himself.

"At what conclusions should I arrive, if I had planted my trees on the opposite side?"

From the reasoning which would have ensued, the following truth would most certainly have been revealed.

"If I were in the other man's place, I should certainly think as he does."

This premise once laid down, the conclusion would be reached; all the more exact, because, without abandoning their arguments, each one would present those which it is easy to turn against an adversary.

Before solving a problem, he who desires to avoid making a mistake must never fail to ask himself this question:

What should I do if my interests were those of the opposite party? Or, yet again:

What should I reply if my adversaries used the same language to me as I purpose using when addressing them?

This method is valuable in that it raises unexpected objections, which the mind would not consider if one had simply studied the question from one's own point of view.

It is a self-evident fact that, according to the state of mind in which we are, things assume different proportions in the rendering of judgement on them.

We must not argue as children do, who, not having the sense of calculating distances, ask how the man standing near to them will be able to enter his house, which they see far away, and which seems to them of microscopic dimensions.

One departs from common sense when one attributes to insignificant things a fundamental value.

We neglect to consider it in a most serious way when we adopt principles contrary to the general consensus of opinion accredited in the environment in which we are living.

"A high dignitary of the court," says Yoritomo, "would be lacking in common sense if he wished to conduct himself as a peasant and, on the other hand, a peasant would give a proof of great folly were he to attempt the remodeling of his life on the principles adopted by courtiers.

"He who, passing his life in camps, wished to think and to act like the philosopher, whose books are his principal society, would cause people to doubt his wisdom; and the thinker who should adopt publicly the methods of a swashbuckler would only inspire contempt."

In ordinary life, one ought to consider this faculty of common sense as the ruling principle of conduct.

One can be lacking in thought, in audacity, in brilliant qualities, if only one possesses common sense.

It takes the place of intelligence in many people, whose minds, unaccustomed to subtle argument, only lend themselves to very simple reasoning.

A versatile mentality rarely belongs to such minds, because it is not their forte to unfold hidden truths.

It walks in the light and keeps in the very middle of the road, far from the ambushes which may be concealed by the hedges of the crossroads.

Many people gifted with common sense but deprived of ordinary intelligence have amassed a fortune, but never, no matter how clever he may be, has a man known success,

THE UTILITY OF COMMON SENSE IN DAILY LIFE

if he has not strictly observed the laws of common sense.

It is not only in debates that the presence of this virtue should make itself felt, but every act of our life should be impregnated with it.

There are no circumstances, no matter how insignificant they may appear, where the intervention of common sense would be undesirable.

It is only common sense which will indicate the course of conduct to be pursued, so as not to hurt the feelings or offend the prejudices of other people.

There are great savants, whose science, freed from all puerile beliefs, rises above current superstition.

They would consider it a great lack of common sense if they expounded their theories before the humble-minded, whose blind faith would be injured thereby.

Of two things one is certain: either they would refuse to believe such theories and this display of learning would be fruitless, or their habitual credulity would be troubled and they would lose their tranquility without acquiring a conviction sufficiently strong to give them perfect peace of mind.

Even in things which concern health, common sense is applicable to daily life.

It is common sense which will preserve us from excesses, by establishing the equilibrium of the annoyances which result from them, with reference to the doubtful pleasure which they procure.

Thanks to common sense, we shall avoid the weariness of late nights and the danger of giving oneself up to the delights of dissipation.

COMMON SENSE: HOW TO EXERCISE IT

"It is common sense," says the philosopher, "which forces us at a banquet to raise our eyes to the hourglass to find out how late it is.

"It is under the inspiration of this great quality of mind that we shall avoid putting to our lips the cup already emptied many times.

"Common sense will reflect upon the mirror of our imagination the specter of the day after the orgy; it will evoke the monster of the headache which works upon the suffering cranium with its claws of steel; and, at some future day, it will show us precocious decrepitude as well as all bodily ills which precede the final decay of those who yield to their passions. It will also impose upon us the performance of duty under the form which it has adopted for each individual.

"Common sense represents for some the care of public affairs; for others those of the family; for us all the great desire to leave intact to our descendants the name which we have received from our fathers.

"For some of those still very young, it is like a lover long desired! "For sages and warriors, it blows the trumpet of glory.

"Finally, common sense is the chosen purpose of every one, courted, demanded, desired or accepted, but it exists, and under the penalty of most serious inconveniences it does not permit us to forget its existence."

Coming down from the heights where he allows himself to be transported at times for a brief moment, Yoritomo tells us the part played by common sense with reference to health.

"Common sense" he assures us, "is the wisest physician whom it is possible to consult.

"If we followed its advice, we should avoid the thousand and one little annoyances of illnesses caused by imprudence.

"The choice of clothing would be regulated according to the existing temperature.

"One would avoid the passing at once from extreme heat to extreme cold.

"One would never proffer this stupid reflection: Bah! I shall take care of myself, which impudent people declare when exposing themselves carelessly to take cold.

"We should understand that disease is a cause of unparalleled disorder and discord.

"In addition to the thought of possible sufferings, that of grief for those whom we love, joined to the apprehension of a cessation of social functions, on whose achievement depends our fortune, would suffice to eliminate all idea of imprudence, if we had the habit of allowing common sense to participate in all our actions of daily life.

"To those who walk under its guidance; it manifests itself without ceasing; it dominates all actions without their being compelled to separate themselves from it.

"It is unconsciously that they appeal to common sense and they have no need of making an effort to follow its laws.

"Common sense is the intelligence of instinct."

7

POWER OF DEDUCTION

Before entering the path which relates directly to the intellectual efforts concerning the acquisition of common sense, the Shogun calls our attention to the power of deduction.

"It is only," said he, "where we are sufficiently permeated with all the principles of judgement that we shall be able to think of acquiring this quality, so necessary to the harmony of life.

"The most important of all the mental operations which ought to be practised by him who desires common sense to reign supreme in all his actions and decisions, is incontestably deduction.

"When the union of ideas, which judgement permits, is made with perception and exactness, there results always an analysis, which, if practised frequently, will end by becoming almost a mechanical act.

"It is, however, well to study the phases of this analysis, in order to organize them methodically first.

"Later, when the mind shall be sufficiently drilled in this kind of gymnastics, all their movements will be repeated in an almost unconscious way, and deduction, that essential principle of common sense, will be self-imposed.

"In order that deductions may be a natural development, the element relating to those which should be the object of judgement should be grouped first.

"The association of statements is an excellent method for it introduces into thought the existence of productive agents.

"We have already spoken of the grouping of thoughts, which is a more synthetical form of that selection.

"Instead of allowing it to be enlarged by touching lightly on all that which is connected with the subject, it is a question, on the contrary, of confining it to the facts relating to only one object.

"These facts should be drawn from the domain of the past; by comparison, they can be brought to the domain of the present in order to be able to associate the former phenomena with those from which it is a question of drawing deductions.

"It is rarely that these latter depend on one decision alone, even when they are presented under the form of a single negation or affirmation.

"Deduction is always the result of many observations, formulated with great exactness, which common sense binds together.

"That which is called a line of action is always suggested by the analysis of the events which were produced under circumstances analogous to those which exist now.

"From the result of these observations, the habit of thinking permits of drawing deductions and common sense concludes the analysis.

"The method of deduction rests upon this.

"One thing being equal to a previous one should produce the same effects.

"If we find ourselves faced by an incident that our memory can assimilate with another incident of the same kind, we must deduce the following chain of reasoning:

"First, the incident of long ago has entailed inevitable consequences.

"Secondly, the incident of today ought to produce the same effects, unless the circumstances which surround it are different.

"It is then a question of analyzing the circumstances and of weighing the causes whose manifestation could determine a disparity in the results.

"We shall interest ourselves first in the surroundings for thus, as we have said, habits of thought and feeling vary according to the epoch and the environment.

"A comparison will be established between persons or things, in order to be absolutely convinced of their degree of conformity.

"The state of mind in which we were when the previous events were manifested will be considered, and we shall not fail to ascertain plainly the similarity or change of humour at the moment as related to that of the past.

"It is also of importance to observe the state of health, for under the affliction of sickness things assume very easily a hostile aspect.

"It would be wrong to attribute to events judged during an illness the same value which is given to them at this present moment.

POWER OF DEDUCTION

"When one is absolutely decided as to the relation of new perceptions and mental representations, one can calculate exactly the degree of comparison.

"The moment will then have arrived to synthesize all the observations and to draw from them the following deductions:

"First, like causes ought, all things being equal, to produce like effects.

"Secondly, the event which is in question will therefore have the same consequences as the previous one, since it is presented under the same conditions.

"Or again:

"Being granted the principle that like causes produce like effects, as I have just affirmed, and that there exist certain incompatibilities between the contingencies of the past and those of today, one must allow that these incompatibilities will produce different results.

"And, after this reasoning, the deductions will be established by constituting a comparison in favour of either the present or past state of things."

But the philosopher, who thinks of everything, has foreseen the case where false ideas have obscured the clearness of the deductions, and he said to us:

"The association of false ideas, if it does not proceed from the difficulty of controlling things, is always in ungovernable opposition to the veracity of the deduction.

"What would be thought of a man of eighty years who, coming back to his country after a long absence, said, on seeing the family roof from a distance:

"'When I was twenty years old, in leaving here, it took

me twenty minutes to reach the home of my parents, so I shall reach the threshold in twenty minutes.'

"The facts would be exact in principle.

"The distance to be covered would be the same; but legs of eighty years have not the same agility as those of very young people, and in predicting that he will reach the end of his walk in the same number of minutes as he did in the past, the old man would deceive himself most surely.

"If, on the contrary, on reaching the same place he perceived that a new route had been made, and that instead of a roundabout way of approach, as in the past, the house was now in a straight line from the point where he was looking at it, it would be possible to estimate approximately the number of minutes which he could gain on the time employed in the past, by calculating the delay imposed upon him by his age and his infirmities.

"Those to whom deduction is familiar, at times astonish thoughtless persons by the soundness of their judgement.

"A prince drove to his home in the country in a sumptuous equipage.

"He was preceded by a herald and borne in a palanquin by four servants, who were replaced by others at the first signs of fatigue, in order that the speed of the journey should never be slackened.

"As they were mounting, with great difficulty, a zigzag road which led up along the side of a hill, one of these men cried out:

"'Stop,' said he, 'in the name of Buddha, stop!'

"The prince leaned out from the palanquin to ask the cause of this exclamation: "'My lord,' cried the man, 'if you care to live, tell your porters to stop!'

"The great man shrugged his shoulders and turning toward his master of ceremonies, who was riding at his side, said:

"'See what that man wants.'

"But scarcely had the officer allowed his horse to take a few steps in the direction of the man who had given warning when the palanquin, with the prince and his bearers, rolled down a precipice, opened by the sinking in of the earth.

"They raised them all up very much hurt, and the first action of the prince, who was injured, was to have arrested the one who, according to him, had evoked an evil fate.

"He was led, then and there, to the nearest village and put into a cell. "The poor man protested.

"'I have only done what was natural,' said he. 'I am going to explain it, but I pray you let me see the prince; I shall not be able to justify myself when he is ill with fever.'

"'What do you mean,' they replied, 'do you prophesy that the prince will have a fever?'

"'He is going to have it.'

"'You see, you are a sorcerer,' said the jailer, 'you make predictions.'

"And then he shut him in prison, to go away and to relate his conversation to them all.

"During this time, they called in a healer who stated that the wounds of the great nobleman were not mortal in themselves, but that the fever which had declared itself could become dangerous.

"He was cured after long months.

"During this time the poor man languished in his prison,

from whence he was only taken to appear before the judges.

"Accused of sorcery and of using black magic, he explained very simply that he had foreseen the danger, because in raising his eyes he had noticed that the part of the ground over which the herald had passed was sinking, and that he had drawn the following conclusions:

"The earth seemed to have only a medium thickness.

"Under the feet of the herald he had seen it crumble and fall in.

"He had deduced from this that a weight five times as heavy added to that of the palanquin, would not fail to produce a landslide.

"As to the prediction concerning the fever, it was based on what he had seen when in the war.

"He had then observed that every wound is always followed by a disposition to fever; he therefore could not fail to deduce that the serious contusions occasioned by the fall of the prince would produce the inevitable consequences.

"The judge was very much imprest with the perspicacity of this man; not only did he give him his liberty, but he engaged him in his personal service and in due time enabled him to make his fortune."

We do not wish to affirm—any more than Yoritomo, for that matter—that fortunate deductions are always so magnificently rewarded as were those of this man.

However, without the causes being so striking, many people have owed their fortune to the faculty which they possess of deducing results where the analogy of the past circumstances suggested to them what would happen.

He warns us against the propensity which we have of

too easily avoiding a conclusion which does not accord with our desires.

"Too many people," said he, "wish to undertake to make deductions by eliminating the elements which deprive them of a desired decision.

"They do not fail either to exaggerate the reasons which plead in favour of this decision; also we see many persons suffer from reasoning, instead of feeling the good effects of it."

Those who cultivate common sense will never fall into this error, for they will have no difficulty in convincing themselves that by acting thus they do not deceive any one except themselves.

By glossing over truth in order to weaken the logical consequences of deductions they are the first to be the victims of this childish trick.

That which is called false deduction is rarely aught save the desire to escape a resolution which a just appraisement would not fail to dictate.

It might be, also, that this twisting of judgement comes from a person having been, in some past time, subjected to unfortunate influences.

By devoting oneself to the evolution of thought, of which we have already spoken when presenting the symbolical fan, and above all, by adopting the precepts which, following the method of Yoritomo, we are going to develop in the following lessons, we shall certainly succeed in checking the errors of false reasoning.

"The important thing," said he, "is not to let wander the thought, which, after resting for a moment on the subject with which we are concerned and after touching lightly on ideas of a similar character, begins to stray very far from its basic principles.

"Have you noted the flight of certain birds?

"They commence by gathering at one point, then they describe a series of circles around this point, at first very small, but whose circumference enlarges at every sweep.

"Little by little the central point is abandoned, they no longer approach it, and disappear in the sky, drawn by their fancy toward another point which they will leave very soon.

"The thoughts of one who does not know how to gather them together and to concentrate them are like these birds.

"They start from a central point, then spread out, at first without getting far from this centre, but soon they lose sight of it and fly toward a totally different subject that a mental representation has just produced.

"And this lasts until the moment when, in a sudden movement, the first one is conscious of this wandering tendency.

"But it is often too late to bring back these wanderers to the initial idea, for, in the course of their circuits, they have brushed against a hundred others, which are confounded with the first, weaken it, and take away its exact proportions.

"The great stumbling-block again is that of becoming lost in the details whose multiplicity prevents us from discerning their complete function in the act of practising deduction.

"It is better, in the case where our perception finds itself assailed by the multitude of these details, to proceed by the process of elimination, in order not to become involved in useless and lazy efforts.

"In this case we must act like a man who must determine

the colour of a material at a distance where the tiny designs stand out in a relief of white on a background of black.

"Suppose that he is placed at a distance too great to perceive this detail. "What should he do to be able to give the best possible description? "He will proceed by elimination.

"The material is neither red nor green; orange and violet must be set aside, as well as all the subordinate shades.

"It has a dull appearance, hence, it is gray; unless.... And here mental activity comes into play and will suggest to him that gray is composed of black and white.

"He will then be sure to form a judgement which will not be spoiled by falsity, if he declares that the material is a mixture of black and white.

"Later, by drawing nearer, he will be able to analyse the designs and to convince himself of their respective form and colour, but by deducing that the material was made up of the mixture of two colours he will have come as near as possible to the truth:

"Deduction never prejudges; it is based on facts; only on things accomplished; it unfolds the teaching that we ought to obtain as a result."

Again the Shogun recommends to us the union of thoughts and the continuous examination of past incidents in the practise of deductions.

"If on entering a room," said he, "we are at times confused, it happens also that we correct this impression after a more attentive examination.

"The gilding is of inferior quality; the materials are of cotton, the paintings ordinary, and the mattings coarse.

"At first sight we should have deduced, judging from

appearances, that the possessor of this house was a very rich man, but a second examination will cause us to discover embarrassment and anxiety.

"It is the same with all decisions that we must make.

"Before devoting ourselves to deductions inspired by the general aspect of things, it is well to examine them one by one and to discover their defects or recognize their good qualities.

"We shall be able thus to acquire that penetration of mind whose development, by leading us toward wise deductions, will bring us to the discovery of the truth."

8

HOW TO ACQUIRE COMMON SENSE

Common Sense is a science, whatever may be said; according to Yoritomo, it does not blossom naturally in the minds of men; it demands cultivation, and the art of reasoning is acquired like all the faculties which go to make up moral equilibrium.

"This quality," said the philosopher, "is obscure and intangible, like the air we breathe.

"Like the air we breathe, it is necessary to our existence, it surrounds us, envelops us, and is indispensable to the harmony of our mental life.

"To acquire this precious gift, many conditions are obligatory, the principle ones being:

"Sincerity of perception.

"Art of the situation.

"Attention.

"Approximation.

"Experience.

"Comparison.

"Analysis.

"Synthesis.

"Destination.

"Direction.

"And lastly the putting of the question.

"It is very clear that without exactness of perception we could not pretend to judge justly; it would then be impossible for us to hear the voice of common sense, if we did not strive to develop it.

"Perception is usually combined with what they call in philosophical language adaptation.

"Otherwise it is difficult, when recognizing a sensation, not to attribute it at once to the sentiment which animated it at the time of its manifestation.

"The first condition, then, in the acquiring of common sense is to maintain perfection in all its pristine exactness, by abstracting the contingencies which could influence us.

"If we do not endeavor to separate from our true selves the suggestions of sense-consciousness, we shall reach the point where perception is transformed into conception, that is to say, we shall no longer obtain reality alone, but a modified reality.

"With regard to perception, if we understand its truthfulness; it will be a question for reawakening it, of placing ourselves mentally in the environment where it was produced, and of awakening the memory, so as to be able to distinguish, without mistake, the limits within which it is narrowly confined.

"The art of situation consists in reproducing, mentally, past facts, allowing for the influence of the surroundings at that time, as compared with the present environment.

HOW TO ACQUIRE COMMON SENSE

"One must not fail to think about the influences to which one has been subjected since this time.

"It is possible that life during its development in the aspirant to common sense may have changed the direction of his first conceptions either by conversation or by reading or by the reproduction of divers narrations.

"It would then be a lack of common sense to base an exact recollection of former incidents on the recent state of being of the soul, without seeking to reproduce the state of mind in which one was at the epoch when those incidents occurred.

"Activity of mind, stimulated to the utmost, is able to give a colour to preceding impressions, which they never have had, and, in this case again, the recollection will be marred by inexactness.

"The art of situation requires the strictest application and on this account it is a valuable factor in the acquirement of common sense.

"Attention vitalizes our activity in order to accelerate the development of a definite purpose toward which it can direct its energy.

"It could be analysed as follows:

"First, to see; "Secondly, to hear.

"The functions of the other senses come afterward, and their susceptibility can attract our attention to the sensations which they give us, such as the sense of smell, of touch, of taste.

"These purely physical sensations possess, however, a moral signification, from which we are permitted to make valuable deductions.

"The first two have three distinct phases:

"First degree, to see. "Second degree, to look. "Third degree, to observe.

"If we see a material, its colour strikes us first and we say: I have seen a red or yellow material, and this will be all.

"Applying ourselves more closely, we look at it and we define the peculiarities of the colour. We say: it is bright red or dark red.

"In observing it we determine to what use it is destined.

"The eye is attracted by:

"The colour.

"The movement.

"The form. "The number. "The duration.

"We have just spoken of the colour.

"The movement is personified by a series of gestures that people make or by a series of changes to which they subject things.

"The form is represented by the different outlines. "The number by their quantity.

"The duration by their length; one will judge of the length of time it takes to walk a road by seeing the length of it.

"The act of listening is divided into three degrees. "First degree, to hear.

"Second degree, to understand. "Third degree, to reflect.

"If some one walking in the country hears a dog bark he perceives first a sound: this is the act of hearing.

"He will distinguish that this sound is produced by the barking of a dog; this is the act of understanding.

"Reflection will lead him then to think that a house or a human being is near, for a dog goes rarely alone.

"If the things which are presented to our sight are complex, those which strike our ears are summed up in one word, sound, which has only one definition, the quality of the sound.

"Then follow the innumerable categories of sound that we distinguish only by means of comprehension and reflection, rendered so instinctive by habit that we may call them automatic, so far as those which relate to familiar sounds.

"The example which we have just given is a proof of this fact.

"Let us add that this habit develops each sensitive faculty to its highest degree.

"The inhabitants of the country can distinguish each species of bird by listening to his song; and the hermits, the wanderers, those who live with society on a perpetual war footing, perceive sounds which would not strike the ears of civilized people.

"Approximation is also one of the stones by whose aid we construct the edifice of common sense.

"Concerning the calculations of probabilities, the application of approximation will allow us to estimate the capacity or the probable duration of things.

"We can not say positively whether a man will live a definite number of years but we can affirm that he will never live until he is two hundred.

"There are, for approbation, certain known limits which serve as a basis for the construction of reasoning, inspired by common sense.

"It can be affirmed, in a positive way, that, if the trunk of a tree were floating easily, without sinking to the bottom of the water, it would not float the same if thirty men were to ride astride of it.

"The initial weight of the tree permits it to maintain itself on the surface; but if it be increased to an exaggerated total, we can, without hesitation, calculate indirectly the moment when it will disappear, dragging with it the imprudent men who trusted themselves to it.

"Everything in life is a question of approximation.

"The house which is built for a man will be far larger than the kennel, destined to shelter a dog, because the proportions have been calculated, by approximation, according to the relative difference between the stature of the human and canine species.

"Clothing is also suited to the temperature.

"One naturally thinks that, below a certain degree of cold, it is necessary to change light clothes for those made of thicker material.

"As with the majority of the constructive elements of common sense, approximation is always based on experience.

"It draws its conclusions from the knowledge of known limitations, whose affirmation serves as a basis for the argument which determines deduction in a most exact manner.

"Experience itself depends on memory, which permits us to recall facts and to draw our conclusions from them, on which facts reasoning is based."

The Shogun does not fail to draw our attention to the difference between experience and experimentation.

"This last," said he, "only serves to incite the manifestation of the first.

"It consists of determining the production of a phenomenon whose existence will aid us in establishing the underlying principles of an observation which interprets the event.

"That is what is called experience.

"Comparison is a mental operation which permits us to bring things that we desire to understand to a certain point.

"It is comparison which has divided time according to periods, which the moon follows during its entire length.

"It is by comparing their different aspects and by calculating the duration of their transformations, that men have been able to divide time as they do in all the countries of the world.

"The science of numbers is also born of comparison, which has been established between the quantities that they represent.

"This is the art of calculating the differences existing between each thing, by determining the relativeness of their respective proportions.

"Comparison acts on the mind automatically, as a rule.

"It is indispensable to the cultivation of common sense, for it furnishes the means of judging with full knowledge of all the circumstances.

"Analysis is an operation, which consists of separating each detail from the whole and of examining these details separately, without losing sight of their relationship to the central element.

"Analysis of the same object, while being scrupulously exact, can, however, differ materially in its application, according to the way that the object is related to this or that group of circumstances.

"There are, however, immutable things.

"For example: the letters of the alphabet, the elementary sounds, the colours etc., etc.

"It suffices to quote only these three elements; one can easily understand that the most elaborate manuscript is composed of only a definite number of letters always repeating themselves, whose juxtaposition forms phrases, then chapters, and finally the complete work.

"Music is composed only of seven sounds whose different combinations produce an infinite variety of melodies.

"Elementary colours are only three in number. "All the others gravitate around them.

"Therefore, these same letters, these same notes, these same colours, according to their amalgamation, can change in aspect and cooperate in the production of different effects.

"The same letters can express, according to the order in which they are placed, terror or confidence, joy or grief.

"The same is true of notes and colours.

"Common sense ought then, considering these rules, to know how to analyse all the details and, having done this, to coordinate and to classify them, in order to distinguish them easily.

"Coordination and classification form an integral part of common sense."

And Yoritomo, who delights in reducing the most complex questions to examples of the rarest simplicity, says to us:

"I am supposing that one person says to another, I have just met a negro. The interlocutor, as well as he who mechanically registers this fact, without thinking, gives himself up to analysis and to coordination which always precedes synthesis.

"Without being aware of this mental action, their minds will be occupied first with the operations of perception then of classification.

"This negro was a man of a colour which places him in a certain group of the human race.

"It is always thus that common sense proceeds, its principal merit being to know how to unite present perceptions with those previously cognized, then to understand how to coordinate them so as to be able to group them concretely, that is to say, to synthesize them.

"Destination is defined as the purpose or object, born of deduction and of classification.

"Destination does not permit of losing sight of the end which is proposed.

"It allows the consideration of the purpose to predominate always, and directs all actions toward this purpose, these actions being absolutely the demonstrations of this unique thought.

"Habits, acquired in view of certain realizations, ought to be dropt from the moment the purpose is accomplished, or that it is weakened."

It is by absolutely perpetuating those habits, whose pretext has disappeared, that one sees the achievement of certain actions which have been roughly handled by common sense.

"There are," again says the philosopher, "certain customs, whose origin it is impossible to remember; at the time of their birth, they were engendered by necessity, but even tho their purpose be obliterated, tradition has preserved them in spite of everything, and those who observe them do not take into consideration their absurdity.

"People of common sense refrain from lending themselves to these useless practises, or, if they consent to allow them a place in their thoughts it is that they attribute to them some reason for existence, either practical or sentimental."

Direction is indicated by circumstances, by environment, or by necessity.

There is direction of resolutions as well as direction of a journey; it is necessary, from the beginning, to consider well the choice of a good route, after having done everything possible to discriminate carefully between it and all other routes proposed.

It happens, however, that the way leads also through the cross-roads; it is even indispensable to leave the short cuts in order to trace the outline of the obstacles.

Direction is, then, an important factor in the acquiring of common sense.

The putting of the question takes its character from comparison, from experience, and principally from approximation; but it is in itself a synthesis of all the elements which compose common sense.

He who wishes to acquire common sense should be impregnated with all that has preceded.

Then he will discipline himself, so as to be able to judge, by himself, of the degree of reason which he has the right to assume.

He will begin by evoking some subject, comparing its visual forms with, those forms which he understands the best, in other words, to the perceptions which are the most familiar to him.

If it concerns a question to be solved, he will try to recall some similar subject, and establish harmony, by making them both relative to a common antecedent.

Yoritomo advises choosing simple thoughts for the beginning. "One will say, for example:

"Such a substance is a poison; the seeds of this fruit contain a weak dose of it; these seeds could then become a dangerous food, if one absorbed a considerable quantity.

"Common sense will thus indicate a certain abstaining from eating of it.

"Then one may extend his argument to things of a greater importance, but taking great care to keep within the narrow limits of rudimentary logic.

"One must be impregnated with this principle:

"Two things equal to a third demand an affirmative judgement or decision. "In the opposite case the negative deduction is enjoined.

"It is by deductions from the most ordinary facts that one succeeds in making common sense intervene automatically in all our judgements.

"What would be thought of one who, finding himself in a forest at the time of a violent storm, would reason as follows:

"First: The high summits attract lightning. "Secondly: Here is a giant tree.

"Thirdly: I'm going to take refuge there.

"Then it is that common sense demands that the state his three propositions as follows:

"First: High summits attract lightning. "Secondly: Here is a giant tree.

"Thirdly: I'm going to avoid its proximity because it will surely be dangerous.

"If he acted otherwise; if, in spite of his knowledge of the danger, he took shelter under the branches of the gigantic tree, exposing himself to be struck by lightning, one could, in this case, only reproach him with imprudence and lay the blame to the lack of common sense which allowed him to perform the act that logic condemned."

Now the old Nippon speaks to us of the means to employ, that we may avoid pronouncing too hasty judgements, which are always, of necessity, weakened by a too great indulgence for ourselves and at the same time too great a severity for others.

"I was walking one day," said he, "on the shores of a lake, when I discovered a man sitting at the foot of a bamboo tree, in an attitude of the greatest despair.

"Approaching him, I asked him the cause of his grief.

"'Alas!' said he to me, 'the gods are against me; everything which I undertake fails, and all evils crush me.

"'After the one which has just befallen me only one course of action is left to me, to throw myself in the lake. But I am young, and I am weeping for myself before resolving to take such a step.'

"And he related to me how, after many attempts without success, he had at last gained a certain sum of money, the loss of which he had just experienced.

"In what way did you lose it?" I asked him. "'I put it in this bag.'

"'Has some one stolen it?'

"'No, it has slipt through this rent.'

"And he showed me a bag, whose ragged condition confirmed, and at the same time illustrated his statement.

"'Listen,' said I, sitting down beside him, 'you are simply devoid of common sense, by invoking the hatred of the gods! You alone are the cause of your present misery.

"'If you had simply reasoned before placing your money in this bag, this would not have happened to you.'

"And as he opened his eyes wide:

"'You would have thought this,' I resumed:

"'The material, very much worn, is incapable of standing any weight without tearing.

"'Now, the money which I possess is heavy, my bag is worn out.

"'I shall not, therefore, put my money in this bag or, at least, I shall take care to line it beforehand with a solid piece of leather.

"'From this moment,' I proceeded, 'there only remains one thing for you to do, always consult common sense before coming to any conclusion, and you will always succeed.

"'As for your opinion concerning the hatred of the gods for you, if you will once more call common sense to your assistance you will reason as follows:

"'Gracious divinities protect only wise people. "'Now, I have acted like a fool.

"'It is, therefore, natural that they should turn away from me.'

"How many useless imprecations would be avoided," adds the Shogun, "if it were given to men to know how to employ the arguments which common sense dictates, in order to distribute the weight of the mistakes committed among those who deserve the burden, without, at the same time, forgetting to assume our own share of the responsibility if we have erred.

"Nothing is more sterile than regrets or reproaches when they do not carry with them the resolution never again to fall into the same error."

Afterward the philosopher demonstrates to us the necessity of abstracting all personality from the exercises which combine for the attainment of common sense.

"There is," said he, "an obstacle against which all stupid people stumble; it is the act of reasoning under the influence of passion.

"Those who have not decided to renounce this method of arguing will never be able to give a just decision.

"There are self-evident facts, which certain people refuse to admit, because this statement of the truth offends their sympathies or impedes their hatreds, and they force themselves to deny the evidence, hoping thus to deceive others regarding it.

"But truth is always the strongest and they soon become the solitary dupes of their own wilful blindness.

"The man of common sense knows how to recognize falsehood wherever he meets it; he knows how vain it is to conceal a positive fact and also how dangerous it is to deceive oneself, a peril which increases in power, in proportion to the effort made to ignore it.

"He does not wish to imitate those pusillanimous people who prefer to live in the agony of doubt rather than to look

HOW TO ACQUIRE COMMON SENSE

misfortunes in the face. He who is determined to acquire common sense will use the following argument:

"Doubt is a conflict between two conclusions.

"So long as it exists it is impossible to adopt either.

"Serenity is unknown to those whom doubt attacks.

"To obtain peace, it is necessary to become enlightened.

"However, it is wise always to foresee the least happy issue and to prepare to support the consequences.

"The man who thinks thus will be stronger than adversity and will know how to struggle with misfortune without allowing it to master him."

It is in these terms that Yoritomo initiates us into what he calls the mechanism of common sense; in other words, the art of acquiring by the simplest reasoning this quality dull as iron, but, like it, also solid and durable.

9

COMMON SENSE AND ACTION

These qualities are two relatives very near of kin; but, just for this reason, they must not be confounded.

While common sense is applied to all the circumstances of life, practical sense is applicable to useful things.

Common sense admits a very subtle logic which is, at times, a little complex.

Practical sense reasons, starting from one point only; viz., material conveniences.

It is possible for this sense to be spoiled by egotism, if common sense does not come to its assistance.

It is by applying the discipline of reasoning to practical sense that it modifies simple sense perception by urging it to ally itself with logic, which unites thought to sentiment and reason.

"The association of common sense and practical sense is necessary," says Yoritomo, "in order to produce new forms, at the same time restraining the imagination within the limits of the most exact deductions and of the most impartial judgement."

Science is, in reality, a sort of common sense to which the rules of reasoning are applied, and is supported by arguments which practical sense directs into productive channels.

That which is called great common sense is none other than a quality with which people are endowed who show great mental equilibrium whenever it is a question of resolving material problems.

These people are generally country people or persons of humble position, whose physical organism has been developed without paying much attention to their intellectual education; they are, in fact, perfect candidates for the attainment of common sense, without having been educated to this end.

Their aptitude results from a constant habit of reflection which, rendering their attention very keen, has permitted them to observe the most minute details, therefore they can form correct conclusions, when it is a question of things that are familiar to them.

A peasant who has been taught by nature will be more skilled in prophesying about the weather than others.

He will also know how to assign a limit to the daily working hours, at the same time stating the maximum time which one can give without developing repulsion, which follows excesses of all kinds.

In his thought, very simple, but very direct, will be formulated this perfect reasoning:

Health is the first of all blessings, since without it we are incapable of appreciating the other joys of life.

If I compromise this possession I shall be insensible to all others.

It is, therefore, indispensable that I should measure my

efforts, for, admitting that a certain exaggerated labour brings me a fortune, I shall not know how to enjoy it if illness accompanies it.

This is the logic which is called practical sense.

Yoritomo continues, saying that there is a very close connection between the faculty of judging and that of deducing.

"Practical sense, allied to common sense, comes to the assistance of the latter, when it is tempted to reject the chain of analogy, whose representation too often draws one far from the initial subject.

"It facilitates coordination, clearness, and precision of thought.

"It knows how to consider contingencies, and never fails to have a clear understanding of relative questions."

And to illustrate his theory, he cites us an example which many of our young contemporaries would do well to remember.

"There was," said he, "in the village of Fu-Isher, a literary man, who wrote beautiful poems.

"He lived in great solitude, and no one would have heard of his existence if it had not been that my master, Lang-Ho, while walking in the woods one day, was attracted by the harmonious sounds of poetry, which this young man was reciting, without thinking that he had any other listeners than the birds of the forest.

"Lang-Ho made himself known to him and began to question him.

"He learned that he did not lack ambition, but, being poor, and having no means of approaching those who would have been able to patronize him, he was singing of nature for his own pleasure, waiting patiently until he should be able to influence the powerful ones of the earth to share his appreciation.

"Lang-Ho, touched by his youth and his ardor, pointed out to him the dwelling of a prince, a patron of the arts, and, at the same time, told him how he ought to address the nobleman, assuring him that the fact of his being a messenger from a friend of the prince would open the doors of the palace to him.

"The next day the young poet presented himself at the home of the great lord, who, knowing that he had been sent by Lang-Ho, received him in spite of the fact that he was suffering intensely from a violent headache.

"He learned from the young man that he was a poet and treated him with great consideration, making him understand, however, that all sustained mental effort was insupportable to him on that day.

"But the poet, not paying attention to the prince's exprest desire, unrolled his manuscripts and began reading an interminable ode without noticing the signs of impatience shown by his august hearer.

"He did not have the pleasure of finishing it.

"The prince, seeing that the reader did not understand his importunity, struck a gong and ordered the servant who appeared to conduct the young man out of his presence.

"Later, he declared to Lang-Ho that his protege had no talent at all, and reprimanded him severely for having sent the poet to the palace.

"But my master did not like to be thus criticized.

"So, a little while after that, one day, when that same prince was in an agreeable frame of mind, Lang-Ho invited him to the reading of one of his works.

"The nobleman declared that he had never heard anything more beautiful.

"'That is true,' said Lang-Ho, 'but you ought to have said this the first time you heard it.'

"And he revealed to the prince that these verses were those of the young man whom he had judged so harshly."

From this story two lessons may be drawn:

The first is, that if common sense indicates that judgement should not change from scorn to enthusiasm, when it is a question of the same object, practical sense insists that one should be certain of impartiality of judgement, by avoiding the influence of questions which relate to environment and surrounding circumstances.

The second concerns opportunity.

We have already had occasion to say how much some things, which seem desirable at certain times, are questionable when the situation changes.

Bad humour creates ill will; therefore it is abominably stupid to provoke the manifestation of the second when one has proved the existence of the first.

In order that there may be a connection between the faculty of judgement and that of deduction, it is essential that nothing should be allowed to interpose itself between these two phases of the argument.

Harmony between all judgements is founded on common sense, but it is practical common sense, which indicates this harmony with precision.

COMMON SENSE AND ACTION

It is also practical common sense which serves as a guide to the orator who wishes to impress his audience.

He will endeavor first to choose a subject which will interest those who listen to him.

In this endeavor he ought, above all, to consult opportunity.

And, as we have remarked on many occasions, the Shogun expresses theories on this subject, to which the people of the twentieth century could not give too much earnest consideration.

"There are," said he, "social questions, as, for example, dress and custom.

"With time, opinions change, as do forms and manners, and this is quite reasonable.

"The progress of science by ameliorating the general conditions of existence, introduces a need created by civilization which rejects barbarous customs; the mentality of a warrior is not that of an agriculturist; the man who thinks about making his possessions productive has not the same inclinations as he whose life is devoted to conquest, and the sweetness of living in serenity, by modifying the aspirations, metamorphoses all things.

"In order to lead attention in the direction which is governed by reason, it is indispensable for the orator that he should expound a subject whose interpretation will satisfy the demand of opportunity, which influences every brain.

"Practical sense will make him take care to speak only of things that he has studied thoroughly.

"It will induce him to expound his theory in such a way that his hearers will have to make no effort to assimilate it.

"That which is not understood is easily criticized, and practical sense would prevent an orator from attempting to establish an argument whose premises would offend common sense.

"He would be certain of failure in such a case.

"His efforts will be limited, then, to evoking common sense, by employing practical sense, so far as what refers to the application of principles which he desires to apply successfully."

Yoritomo recommends this affiliation for that which concerns the struggle against superstition.

"Superstition," he says, "offends practical sense as well as common sense, for it rests on an erroneous analysis.

"Its foundation is always an observation marred by falsity, establishing an association between two facts which have nothing in common.

"There are people who reenter their homes if, when they reach the threshold, they perceive a certain bird; others believe that they are threatened with death if they meet a white cat."

Without going back to the days of Yoritomo, we shall find just as many people who are the victims of superstitions concerning certain facts, which are only the observance of customs fallen into disuse, and whose practise has been perpetuated through the ages, although, as we have said in the preceding chapter, the purpose of the custom has disappeared, but the custom itself has not been forgotten.

It is in this way that the origin of the superstition concerning salt dates back to the time of the Romans, who (while at variance with the principles of contemporary agriculture) sowed salt in the fields of their enemies and thought that by so doing they would make them sterile.

To that far-distant epoch can be traced the origin of the superstition concerning the spilling of salt.

Whatever may have been its cause, superstition is the enemy of common sense, for, when it does not originate in an abolished custom, it is the product of a personal impression, associating two ideas absolutely unconnected.

"Practical sense," Yoritomo continues, "is a most valuable talent to cultivate, for it prevents our judging from appearances.

"Frivolous minds are always inclined to draw conclusions from passing impressions; they adopt neither foresight, nor precaution, nor approximation.

"There are people who will condemn a country as utterly unattractive, because they happened to have visited it under unfavourable circumstances.

"Others, without considering what a country has previously produced, and that at present the grain has not been planted, will declare unfertile the soil which has been untilled for some months.

"On the other hand, if they visit a house on a sunny day, it would be impossible for them to associate it with the idea of rain.

"It would be most difficult to make these people alter their judgement, prematurely formed, and, in spite of the most authoritative assertions and the most self-evident proofs, their initial idea will dominate all those which one would like to instil into their minds.

"One moment would, however, suffice for reason to convince them that the variations of atmosphere and the conditions of cultivation can modify the aspect of a country, of a field, and of a house, to the extent of giving them an appearance totally different from the one which they seemed to have.

"But he who judges by appearances never rejoices in the possession of that faculty which may be called reason in imagination.

"This is a gift, developed by practical sense and which common sense happily directs in right channels.

"Those who are endowed with this faculty can, with the help of reasoning, and by means of thought, build up a future reality based on a judgement whose affirmation admits of no doubt.

"It is not a question of hypothesis, no matter how well-founded it is.

"Experience, in this case, is united with deduction to form a preconceived but certain idea.

"By cultivating practical sense, we shall escape the danger of idealization which, with people of unbalanced mentality, often sheds an artificial light upon the picture."

There is still another point to which Yoritomo calls our attention, in order to encourage us to cultivate the twin reasoning powers whose advantages we are trying to commend in this chapter:

"Practical sense," says he, "sometimes puts common sense apparently in the wrong, while acting, however, without the inspiration of the latter.

"This happens when it is an advantage, for the perfect equilibrium of the projects in question, that it should be maintained at the same pitch, in order that it may be understood by all.

"In the legendary days, snow the colour of fire once fell on the inhabitants of a little village, who were all about to attend a religious ceremony.

"One man alone, an old philosopher, had remained at home because, at the time they were to leave, he suddenly fell ill.

"When his sufferings were relieved, he started out to join the others and found them committing all sorts of follies.

"Two among them were reviling one another, each one claiming that he was the only king.

"Some were weeping because they thought that they were changed into beasts.

"Others were screaming, without rime or reason, now embracing each other, now attacking one another furiously.

"Soon the wise man recognized that they had been affected by the fall of snow, which had made them crazy, and he tried to speak to them in the language of reason.

"But all these crazy people turned on him, crying out that he had just lost his reason and that he must be shut away.

"They undertook the task of taking him back to his home, but, as that was not to be accomplished without rough usage, he assumed the part indicated by practical sense; this man of common sense feigned insanity, and from the moment the insane people thought that he resembled them they let him alone and ceased to torment him.

"The philosopher profited by this fact to disarm their excitement, and, little by little, all the time indulging in a thousand eccentricities, which had no other object than to protect himself against them, he demonstrated their aberration to them."

Could not this story serve as an example to the majority of contemporary critics?

Is it not often necessary to appear to be denuded of common sense, to make the voice of reason dominate?

In the fable of Yoritomo, his philosopher proved his profound knowledge of the human heart, while he put in practise the power of practical sense in apparent opposition, however, to common sense.

We said this at the opening of the chapter: practical sense and common sense are two very near relatives, but they are two and not one.

10

THE MOST THOROUGH BUSINESS MAN

One of the principle advantages of common sense is that it protects the man who is gifted with it from hazardous enterprises, the risky character of which he scents.

Only to risk when possessing perfect knowledge of a subject is the sure means of never being drawn into a transaction by illusory hopes.

An exact conception of things is more indispensable to perfect success than a thousand other more brilliant but less substantial gifts.

"However," says Yoritomo, "in order to make success our own, it is not sufficient to have the knowledge of things, one must above all know oneself.

"On the great world-stage, each one occupies a place which at the start may not always be in the first rank.

"Nevertheless, work, intelligence, directness of thought and, above all, common sense, can exert a positive influence on the future superiority of the situation.

"Before everything else, it is indispensable that we should never delude ourselves about the position which we occupy.

"To define it exactly, one should call to mind the wise adage which says: Know thyself.

"But this knowledge is rare.

"Presumptuous persons readily imagine that they attract the eyes of every one, even if they be in the last rank.

"Timid persons will hide themselves behind others and, notwithstanding, they are very much aggrieved not to be seen.

"Ambitious persons push away the troublesome ones, in order that they themselves may get the first places.

"Lazy persons just let them do it.

"Irresolute persons hesitate before sitting down in vacant places and are consumed with regrets from the time they perceive that others, better prepared, take possession of them; the more so as they no longer get back their own, for, during their hesitation, another has seated, himself there.

"Enthusiasts fight to reach the first rank, but are so fatigued by their violent struggles that they fall, tired out, before they have attained their object.

"Obstinate people persist in coveting inaccessible places and spend strength without results, which they might have employed more judiciously.

"People of common sense are the only ones who experience no nervous tension because of this struggle.

"They calculate their chances, compute the time, do not disturb themselves uselessly, and never abandon their present position until they have a firm grasp on the following place.

"They do not seek to occupy a rank which their knowledge would not permit them to keep; they draw on that faculty with which they are gifted to learn the science of true proportion.

"They do not meddle in endeavors to reform laws; they submit to them, by learning how to adapt them to their needs, and respect them by seeking to subordinate their opinion to the principle on which they are based.

"Persons who have no common sense are the only ones to revolt against the laws of the country where they live.

"The wise man will recognize that they have been enacted to protect him and that to be opposed to their observance would be acting as an enemy to oneself."

However, people will say, if laws are so impeccable in their right to authority, how is it that their interpretation leads so often to disputes?

It is easy to reply that lawsuits are rarely instituted by men of common sense; they leave this burden to people of evil intent, who imagine thus to make a doubtful cause triumph.

It must be conceded that this means succeeds at times with them, when they are dealing with timid or irresolute persons; but those who have contracted the habit of reasoning, and who never undertake anything without consulting common sense, will never allow themselves to be drawn into the by-paths of sophistry.

If they are forced to enter there temporarily, in order to pursue the adversary, who has hidden himself there, they will leave these paths as soon as necessity does not force them to remain there longer and with delight regain the broad road of rectitude.

A few pages further on we find a reflection which the

Shogun, always faithful to his principles of high morality, specially addresses to those who make a profession of humility.

"Obedience," he says, "ought to be considered as a means; but, for the one who wishes to succeed, in no sense can it be honoured as a virtue.

"If it be a question of submission to law, that is nothing else but the performance of a strict duty; this is a kind of compact which the man of common sense concludes with society, to which he promises his support for the maintenance of a protection from which he will be the first to benefit.

"This obedience might be set down as selfishness were it not endorsed by common sense.

"There are people, it is true, who, even although wishing to support their neighbor when called upon to do so by the law, seek to evade this duty if left to themselves.

"These are pirates who have broken completely not only with the spirit of equity, but also with simple common sense.

"It is always foolish to set the example of insubordination, for, if it were followed, it would not be long before general disorder would appear.

"Some men were sitting one day on the edge of an inlet and were trying with a net to catch fish, whose playful movements the men were following through the limpid water.

"According to their character, their perseverance, their cleverness, and the ingenuity of the means employed, they caught a proportionate number of fish; but those who caught the least had one or two.

"This success encouraged them, and they began again in good earnest, each one in his own way, when a stranger appeared; he was armed with a long branch of a tree, which he plunged in the pond, touching the bottom and stirring up the mud, which, as it scattered, rose to the surface of the water.

"The limpidity of the water was immediately changed; one could no longer see the fish, and the fishermen decided to discontinue their sport.

"But the man only laughed at their discomfiture and, brandishing a large net, he threw it in his turn, chaffing them at the patient cunning by which they had, he said, taken such a poor haul.

"He brought up some fish, it is true, but at each haul he was obliged to lose so much time in removing the impurities, the debris, and the weeds of all kinds from the net that very soon the fishermen had the satisfaction of seeing him punished for his mean conduct.

"What he took was scarcely more than what the smartest among them had taken, and his net, filthy from the mud, torn by the roots that he was unable to avoid, was soon good for nothing."

Might it not be from this fable that we have taken the expression, "to fish in troubled waters," of which without a doubt the good Yoritomo furnished the origin many, many centuries ago?

His prophetic mind is unveiled again in the following advice that not a business man of the twentieth century would reject.

"Common sense," he says, "when it is a question of the relations of men as to what concerns business or society, ought to adopt the characteristic of that animal called the chameleon.

"His natural colour is dull, but he has the gift of reflecting the colour of the objects on which he rests.

"Near a leaf, he takes the tint of hope.

"On a lotus, he is glorified with the blue of the sky.

"Is this to say that his nature changes to the point of modifying his natural colour?

"No; he does not cease to possess that which recalls the colour of the ground, and the ephemeral colour which he appropriates is only a semblance, in order that he may be more easily mistaken for the objects themselves.

"The man who boasts of possessing common sense, although preserving his personality, ought not to fail, if he wants to succeed, to reflect that of the person whom he wishes to aid him in succeeding."

Let it not be understood for a moment, that we advise any one to act contrary to the impulses of justice.

But cleverness is a part of common sense in business, and assimilation is essential to success.

It is not necessary to abandon one's convictions in order to reflect principles which, without contradicting them, give them a favourable colour.

Common sense can remain intact and be differently coloured, according as it is applied to the arts, politics, or science.

It would not deserve its name if it did not know how to yield to circumstances, in order to adorn the momentary caprice with flowers of reason.

In the primitive ages, common sense consisted in keeping oneself in a perpetual state of defense; attack was also at times prescribed, by virtue of the principle that it is pernicious to allow one's rights to be imperiled.

Attack was also at times a form of repression.

It was also a lesson in obedience and a reminder not to misunderstand individual rights.

In later times, common sense served to make the advantages of harmony appreciated.

It directed the descendants of peoples exclusively warlike toward the secret place where science unfolds itself to the gaze of the vulgar; then it taught them to provide for their existence by working.

It has demonstrated to them the necessity of reflection, by inciting them to model their present course of life on the lessons which come from the past.

It has given them the means to evoke it easily and effectively.

It has injected into their veins the calmness which permits them to draw just conclusions and to adopt toward preceding reasonings the attitude of absolute neutrality, without which all former presentiments are marred by error.

Each epoch was, for common sense, an opportunity to manifest itself differently.

At the moment when poetry was highly honoured, it would have been unreasonable to have ignored it, for the bards excited great enthusiasm by their songs which gave birth to heroes.

And now, imbued with the principles which in his day might be taken to represent what we today call advanced ideas, Yoritomo continues:

"Common sense can, then, without renouncing its devotion to truth, take various forms or shades, for the truth of yesterday is not always the truth of today.

"The gods of the past are considered simply as idols in our day and the virtues of the distant past would be, at present, moral defects which would prevent men from winning the battle of life, whose ideal is The Best for which all the faculties should strive."

The Shogun also touches lightly on a subject which, already discust in his time, has become, in our day, a burning truth; it is a question of a fault, which in the world of practical life and in that of business can cause considerable injury to him who allows it to be implanted in him.

We refer to that tendency which has been adorned or rather branded successively with the names of hypochondria, pessimism, and lastly neurasthenia, an appellation which comprises all kinds of nervous diseases, the characteristic of which is incurable melancholy.

"There are people," he says, "who are afflicted with a special colour-blindness.

"Everything they look at assumes immediately to their eyes the most sombre hues.

"They see in a flower only the germ of dry-rot; the most ideal beauty appears to them only like the negligible covering of some hideous skeleton.

"However, they hang on to this life which they do not cease to calumniate, and people of common sense are rarely found who will try to reason with them from a common-sense standpoint:

"'Since life is so insupportable to you, why do you impose upon yourself the obligation to struggle with it?

"'Only insane people try to prolong their sojourn in a

place where they suffer martyrdom.'

"It is true that when, perchance, this argument is placed before them, they do not fail to reply by invoking the shame of desertion.

"'Well, is not then the interest of the struggle to which we are subjected a sufficient attraction to keep us at our post?'"

And, always enamored with the doctrine, which we are now assiduously maintaining, he concludes:

"Common sense is, at times, the unfolding of a magnificent force which incites us to attune our environment to actualities.

"One must not, however, fall into excess and draw a huge sword to pierce the clouds, which obscure the sun.

"If struggle is praiseworthy when we have to face a real enemy, it becomes worthy of scorn and laughter if we attack a puerile or imaginary adversary.

"But the number of people incapable of appreciating the true colour of things is not limited to those who enshroud them in black.

"There are others, on the contrary, who obstinately insist upon surrounding them with a halo of sunlight only existing in their imagination.

"For such deluded people, obstacles seen from a distance take on the most attractive appearance; they would be readily disposed to enjoy them and only consent to allow them a certain importance if they absolutely obstruct the way.

"But until the moment when impossibility confronts them, do they deny its existence or underrate its importance by attributing a favourable influence to it.

"This propensity to see all in the ideal would be enviable

if it did not wound common sense, which revenges itself by refusing to these improvident people the help of the reasoning power necessary to sustain them in the crisis of discouragement which brings about irresistibly the establishment of error.

"These unbalanced people rarely experience success, for they are unable, as long as their blindness lasts, to mark out a line of serious conduct for themselves.

"All projects built on the quicksands of false deductions will perish without even leaving behind them material sufficient to reconstruct them.

"It is impossible to combat strongly enough this tendency to self-delusion, which inclines us to become the prey of untruth, by preventing the birth of faith, based on preceding success.

"Sincere conviction, on the contrary, will lead us to refute strongly all the false arguments, which impede thought and would choke it in order to allow unadulterated pleasure to be installed on the ruins of common sense.

"The battle of life demands warriors and conquerors as well as critics, less brilliant, perhaps, but just as worthy of admiration, for their mission is equally important, although infinitely more obscure.

"Whether he be a peasant tilling his field or a rich capitalist manipulating his gold, he who works in order to satisfy the needs or luxury of his existence is a fighter whose hours are spent in occupations more or less dangerous.

"From time to time, however, a cessation of hostilities is produced; such always follows the appearance of common sense which, by giving to things their true proportions, causes the greater part of inequalities to disappear.

"Finally, he who cultivates this virtue unostentatiously will always be protected from the caprices of fortune; if he is poor, common sense will indicate to him the way to cease to be poor, and, if chance has given him birth in opulence, the counsels of experience will demonstrate to him the frailty of possessions that one has not acquired by personal effort."

This conclusion is strikingly true, for it is certain that prosperity attained by personal effort is less likely to fade away than an inherited fortune, whose owner can only understand the ordinary pleasure of a possession which he has not ardently desired.

He who is the maker of his own position is more able to maintain it; he knows the price of the efforts which he had to make in order to construct it, and, armed with common sense, he is as able to defend his treasure as to enjoy the sweet savor of a thing which he has desired, longed for, and won by the force of his will and judgement, placed at the service of circumstances and directed toward success.

11

COMMON SENSE AND SELF-CONTROL

"Where life manifests itself," says Yoritomo, "antagonism always springs up."

"In the eternal struggle between the individual and social soul, each of which, in its turn, is victorious or vanquished, a truce is declared only if self-control is allied to common sense, in order to maintain the equilibrium between individual sentiment, natural to each one of us, and the ideas of mankind as a whole.

"All classes of society are subject to this law, and, from the proudest prince to the humblest peasant, every one is obliged to harmonize their social duties with their personal obligations.

"Those who understand how to imbibe thoroughly the lessons of common sense, never ignore the fact that morality is always closely related to self-interest.

"If each one of us would observe this rule individual happiness would not be long in creating a harmony from which all men would benefit.

"One thing we should avoid, for the attainment of universal tranquility, and that is the perpetual conflict between individual and social interest.

"The day when each one of us can comprehend that he is a part of this 'all,' which is called society, he will admit that sinning against society may be considered the same as sinning against oneself.

"Passing one day before an immense cabin, built of bamboo, which stood near a rice-plantation, I perceived a man who hid himself from my view, without however being able to escape my notice altogether. I went resolutely to him, to ask him the explanation of his suspicious movement.

"After an unsuccessful attempt to escape, he resigned himself to allow me to approach him, and I understood the reason of his apprehension:

"He was carrying several pieces of bamboo which he had detached from the house. He wanted, he said, to make a little blaze because the dampness was chilling him.

"Without replying to him, I led him by the hand to the place where the branches taken away had left a large space, a kind of opening in the side of the house, through which a keen wind was rushing.

"'Look,' I said to him, 'the blaze that you are going to make will warm you for a few minutes, but, during the whole night the cold wind will freeze you—you and your companions.

"'In order to procure for yourself an agreeable but passing sensation you are going to inflict upon them continued sufferings, of which you can not escape your share.'

"The man hung his head and said: 'I had not thought

of this; I was cold and I allowed myself to be tempted by the anticipated pleasure of warming myself, even if only for a few minutes.'

"And, convinced by common sense, he repaired the harm which he had done, first by reason of selfishness, then by thoughtlessness, but, above all, by lack of self-control.

"To dominate oneself to the point of not allowing oneself to become the slave of miserable contingencies which appear as temptations to self-indulgence, and conceal from their pettiness the beauty of the consistent action—this is only given to the chosen few and can only be understood by those who cultivate common sense."

Is this to say that reasoning should be a school for abnegation. Such a thought is far from our minds.

Neither habitual abnegation nor modesty is among the militant virtues, and for this reason the critics ought often to relegate them to their proper place, which is the last, very close to defects to which they closely approach and among whose ranks one must sometimes go in order to discover them.

But, apart from the question of a sterile abnegation, we must foresee that it may be important not to overestimate one's individual interests, to the visible detriment of the general interest.

This is a fault common to all those who have not been initiated into the practise of self-control by means of reasoning based on solid premises.

They are ready to sacrifice very great interests, which do not seem to concern them directly, for some immediate paltry gratification.

"They act," said the philosopher, "like a peasant who should risk his harvest in order to avoid paying the prince the rent which belongs to him.

"Common sense teaches us that we should call to our assistance self-control, in order to repress the tendencies which tempt men to sacrifice the general interest to some personal and vehement desire.

"Rarely do these people find their advantage in separating themselves from the mass, and the prosperity of the greatest number is always the cradle of individual fortunes."

Leaving questions of primary importance to come to the subtleties of detail in which, he delights, Yoritomo speaks to us of self-control allied to common sense, extolling to us its good effects in practical questions of our every-day life.

"We too often confound," said he, "self-control and liberty.

"We are tempted to believe that a slave can not possess it, inasmuch as it is the special possession of all those to whom riches give a superior position in the world.

"How profound is this error!

"The lowest slave can enjoy this liberty, which is worth all others: self-control, which confers intellectual independence more precious than the most precious of possessions, whereas the most powerful prince may be altogether ignorant of this blessing.

"There are dependent souls who, for want of the necessary strength to escape from vassalage to the external impressions will always drag on, feeble and opprest by the exactions of a mental servitude from which they can not free themselves.

"Others rise proudly, ready to command circumstances,

which they dominate with all the power of their volition governed by reason.

"It is common sense which will guide them in this ascent by keeping them within the limits assigned to those things pertaining to reason and rectitude of mind.

"Before everything, it is well not to forget that this faculty invites those who cultivate it to seek always for exact facts.

"Knowledge, in all its aspects is, then, a perfect educator for those who do not wish to build on the flimsy foundation of approximate truth.

"In pronouncing the word knowledge, we do not wish to speak of abstract studies which are only accessible to a small number; we wish to express the thought of instruction embracing all things, even the most humble and ordinary.

"A man from the city was walking in the country one day, not far from a vast swamp.

"All around it were a few miserable huts, the shelter of some peasants whose business it was to gather the reeds from the borders, weaving them into large baskets to be sold afterward in the neighbouring country.

"Little by little twilight descended, slowly enveloping all things in a mist of ashy gray, and vapours arose from afar over the stagnant water.

"The man from the city trembled, believing that he recognized fantoms in this moving vapour; he sought to flee, but, unfamiliar with the locality, he ran along the side of the swamp without finding the end of it.

"Exhausted from fatigue and trembling with fear, he resolved to knock at one of the cabins.

"He was welcomed by a basket-maker, to whom he related his fright, adding that he was unable to understand how this man found the courage to live in a place haunted in such a terrible way.

"The peasant smiled and explained to the man, whose intellectual culture was, however, infinitely superior to his own, by what phenomenon of evaporation these mirages were produced.

"He demonstrated to him that these fantoms were only harmless vapours, and the city man admired the knowledge which common sense had taught the ignorant one."

And Yoritomo concluded:

"This peasant gave there a proof of what self-control allied to common sense can do.

"Instead of allowing himself to be influenced by appearances, he confined himself to reflection, and observation aided by attention led him to a deduction resting on truth.

"The essential factor of control is cool-headedness, which permits of seeing things in their true light, and forbids us to gild them or to darken them, according to our state of mind at the time."

The Shogun adds:

"Fear, hideous fear, is a sentiment unknown to those whose soul communes with self-control and common sense.

"The first of these qualities will produce a fixt resolution tending to calmness, at the same time that it makes a powerful appeal to cool-headedness, which permits of reflection.

"Fear is always the confession of a weakness which disavows struggle and wishes to ignore the name of adversary.

"Cool-headedness is the evanescent examination of

forces, either physical or intellectual, with reference to supposed danger.

"Without self-control cool-headedness can not exist; but it only develops completely under the influence of common sense which dictates to it the reasons for its existence.

"Cool-headedness, by leaving us our liberty of thought, enlightens us undoubtedly on the nature of danger, at the same time that it suggests to us the way to avoid it, if it really exists.

"There can not be a question of fear for those who possess the faculties of which we have just spoken, for it is well known that, from the moment when the cause of fear is defined it ceases to exist; it becomes stupid illusion or a real enemy.

"In the one case, as in the other, it ought not to excite anxiety any longer, but contempt or the desire to fight it.

"For those whose mind is not yet strong enough to resolve on one or other of these decisions it will be well to take up again the argument indicated in the preceding pages, and to say:

"Either the object of my fear really exists, and, in this case, I must determine its nature exactly, in order to use the proper means first to combat it and then to conquer it.

"Or it is only an illusion, and I am going to seek actively for that which produces it, in order never again to fall into the error of which my senses have just been the dupes."

Looking over these manuscripts, so rich in valuable advice, we find once more the following lines:

"Self-control and cool-headedness are above all necessary to aid in dissimulating impressions.

"It is very bad to allow one of the speakers in a dialogue to read the mind of him who speaks to him like an open book.

"He whose thoughts are imprest vividly on the surface is always placed at a glaring disadvantage.

"The thought of glorifying hypocrisy is far from our minds, for it has nothing to do with the attitude which we recommend.

"The hypocrite strives to assume emotions which he does not feel.

"The man gifted with cool-headedness is intent on never allowing them to be seen.

"It keeps his adversary in ignorance of the effect produced by his reasoning and allows him to take his chance, until the moment when, in spite of this feigned indifference, he reveals himself and permits his mind to be seen.

"Now, to know the designs of a rival, when he is ignorant of those that we have conceived, is one of the essential factors of success.

"In every way, he who is informed about the projects of his adversary walks preceded by a torch of light, while the adversary, if he can not divine his opponent's plans, continues to fight in darkness."

The most elementary common sense counsels then cool-headedness when exchanging ideas, even when the discussion is of quite an amicable nature.

From this habit there will result a very praiseworthy propensity to exercise self-control, which is only a sort of superior cool-headedness.

It is also the cause of a noble pride, because it is more

difficult to win a victory over one's passions than to conquer ordinary enemies, and he who, with the support of common sense, succeeds in ruling himself, can calculate, without arrogance, the hour when he will reign over the minds of others.

12

COMMON SENSE DOES NOT EXCLUDE GREAT ASPIRATIONS

"A very common error," says Yoritomo, "is that which consists in classifying common sense among the amorphous virtues, only applicable to things and to people whose fundamental principle is materiality.

"This is a calumny which is spread broadcast by fools who scatter their lives to the four winds of caprice and extravagance.

"Not only does common sense not exclude beauty, but it really aids in its inception and protects its growth by maintaining the reasons which produced its appearance.

"Without it, the reign of the most admired things would be of short duration, granting that the want of logic had not prevented their production.

"What is there more commendable than the love of work, devotion to science, ambition to succeed?

"Could all this exist if common sense did not intervene to permit the development of the deductions on which are based the resolutions that inspired in us these aspirations.

"But this is not all; without logic, which permits us to give them solidity, the most serious resolutions would soon become nothing but vague projects, shattered as soon as formed.

"In common sense lies the cause and the object of things.

"It is common sense which makes us realize that difference that few persons are willing to analyse, and which lies between judgement and opinion.

"We almost always succeed in readily confounding them, and from this mistake results a too-frequent cause of failures.

"Opinion is a conviction which is capable of modification.

"In addition to this, as it is based on mere indications and probability, it is rarely free from the personal element.

"Opinion depends upon the favourite inclination, upon the mood of the moment, upon sundry considerations, which direct it almost always toward the desired solution.

"Also it depends often on thoughtfulness or on the inexactness of the initial representation, which we are pleased to disguise slightly at first, then little by little to colour in accordance with our desires.

"Falsehood does not necessarily enter into this process of tricking things out; it is, three-quarters of the time, the result of an illusion which we are prone to perpetuate within us.

"We are too often in the position of the three wise men who, while rummaging in an old sarcophagus, discovered a vase whose primitive function they were unable to determine with any certainty.

"One of them was a poet and an idealist. "The second only prized positive things.

COMMON SENSE DOES NOT EXCLUDE GREAT ASPIRATIONS

"The third belonged to the category of melancholy people.

"After a few days devoted to special research work, they met together again in order to communicate to each other their different opinions about the exhumed vase.

"'I have found the secret,' said the first. "'I also,' affirmed the second.

"'I equally have found it,' replied the third.

"And each one based his opinion on preconceived notions which reflected their bent of mind:

"'This vase,' said the first, 'was intended to hold incense, which they burned a that epoch, in the belief that the smoke dispelled the evil spirits.'

"'Nonsense!' cried out the second; 'this vase is a pot which at that time served as a receptacle for keeping spices.'

"'Not so!' insisted the third, 'it is an urn of antiquated design used for receiving tears; that is all.'

"These three serious men were certainly sincere in giving explanations which each one of them declared decisive. They exprest opinions which they believed implicitly and which their respective natures directed irresistibly toward their peculiar bents of mind.

"Judgement, in order to be free from all which is not common sense, ought then to put aside all personal predilections, all desire to form a conclusion to humour our inclinations.

"Absolute impartiality of judgement is one of the rarest gifts and at the same time is the noblest quality which we can possess."

We should then conclude, with the Shogun, that common

sense aids in the production of noble aspirations, and is not concerned only with that which relates to materiality, as so many people would have us understand.

The Nippon philosopher teaches us also the part which he assigns to the habitual practise of goodness.

"We are too easily persuaded," he says, "that goodness, like beauty, is a gift of birth.

"It is time to destroy an error rooted in our minds for too many centuries.

"Goodness is acquired by reasoning and logic, as are so many other qualities, and it is common sense which governs its formation.

"Have we ever reflected over the sum total of annoyances that people, who are essentially wicked, add every day to those imposed upon them by circumstances?

"Are we capable of appreciating the joys of life when impatience makes the nerves vibrate or when anger brandishes its torch in the bends and turns of the brain?

"People who lack goodness are the first to be punished for their defect. Serenity is unknown to them and they live in perpetual agitation, caused by the irritation which they experience on the slightest provocation."

Common sense indicates then in an irrefutable way that there is every advantage in being good.

And Yoritomo proves it to us, by using his favourite syllogism:

"Happiness," he says, "is above all a combination of harmony and absence of sorrow.

"Wickedness, by inspiring us with discontent and anger, disturbs this harmony.

COMMON SENSE DOES NOT EXCLUDE GREAT ASPIRATIONS

"We must, therefore, banish wickedness, that we may cultivate goodness, which is the creator of harmony."

Continuing still further the same argument, he adds:

"Common sense would have the tendency even to make us promise to be good, so as to satisfy our own egotism.

"Goodness creates smiles; to sow happiness around one, is a way of having neither eyes nor heart offended by the sight of people in tears; it is the eliciting of an agreeable joy, whose rays will shed a golden light over our life; is it not more pleasing to hear the ring of laughter than to listen to painful sobs?"

So, we should never lose an opportunity of being good and that without mental reservation.

Gratitude is not the possession of every soul and he who does good may expect to receive ingratitude.

He will not suffer from it, if he has done good, not in the way a creditor does who intends to come on the very day appointed to claim his debt, but as a giver who fulfils his mission from which he is expecting a personal satisfaction, without thinking of any acknowledgment for what he has done.

If the debtor is filled with gratitude, the joy of being good is that much increased.

There is a species of common sense of a particularly noble quality that is called moral sense and which the Shogun defines thus:

"The moral sense is the common sense of the soul; it is the superior power of reasoning which stands before us that we may be prevented from passively following our instincts; it is by its assistance that we succeed without too much difficulty in climbing the steep paths of duty.

"This sense discerns an important quality, which puts us on our guard against the danger of certain theories, whose brilliancy might seduce us.

"It is the moral sense which indicates to us the point of delimitation separating legitimate concessions from forbidden license.

"It allows us to go as far as the dangerous place where the understanding with conscience might become compromised and, by reasoning, proves to us that there would be serious danger in proceeding further.

"It is the moral sense which distinguishes civilized man from the brute; it is the regulator of the movements of the soul and the faithful indicator of the actions which depend on it."

We must really pity those who are deprived of moral sense for they are the prey of all the impulses created in them by the brute nature, which sleeps in the depths of each human creature.

The man whose moral sense is developed will live at peace with himself, for he will only know the evil of doubt when he realizes the satisfaction of having conquered it.

Moral sense, like common sense, is formed by reasoning and is fostered by the practise of constant application.

It is the property of those who avoid evil, as others avoid the spatter of mud, through horror of the stains which result from it.

Those who do not have this apprehension flounder about, cover themselves with mud, sink in it and finally are swallowed up.

COMMON SENSE DOES NOT EXCLUDE GREAT ASPIRATIONS

Yoritomo again takes up the defense of common sense, with reference to the arts.

"Can one imagine," he says, "a painter conceiving a picture and grouping his figures in such a way as to violate the rules of common sense?

"We should be doomed, if this were true, to see men as tall as oak-trees and houses resembling children's toy constructions, placed without reference to equilibrium among green or pink animals, whose legs had queer shapes.

"Madmen represent nature thus, which seems to them outlined in strange forms.

"But people of common sense reproduce things just as sound judgement conceives of them; if they throw around them at times the halo of beauty which seems exaggerated, let us not decry them.

"Beauty exists everywhere; it dwells in the most humble objects, makes all around us resplendent and, if we refuse to see it, we are blinded by an unjust prejudice, or our minds are not open to the faculty of contemplation.

"It is revealed above all to those who cultivate common sense and reject the sophistries of untruth that they may surround themselves with truth.

"Such people scorn trivial casualties; they adopt an immutable rule, reasoning, which permits them to deduce, to judge, and afterward to produce.

"All beautiful creations are derived from this source.

"The most admirable inventions would never have been known if common sense had not helped them to be produced, strengthening those who conceived them by the support of logic, which demonstrated to them the truth of their presumptions.

"Authority follows, based on the experience which, by maintaining the effect of judgement, has armed them with the strength of the mind, the true glory of peaceful conquerors."

Would one not say that the Shogun, in writing these lines, foresaw the magnificent efforts which we are witnessing each day and that from the depths of time he caught a glimpse of these brave conquerors of the air and of space, whose great deeds, seeming at times the result of a crazy temerity, are in reality only homage rendered to common sense, which has permitted them to calculate the value of their initiative without mistake?

And one can not be denied the pleasure of entering once more into close communion of thought with the old philosopher when he says:

"Enthusiasm is of crystal but common sense is of brass."